SAVING ENDANGERED SPECIES

THE GREEN SEA TURTLE

Help Save This Endangered Species!

Marty Fletcher and Glenn Scherer

MyReportLinks.com Books

an imprint of

Enslow Publishers, Inc.

Library of Congress Cataloging-in-Publication Data

Fletcher, Marty.
 The green sea turtle : help save this endangered species! / Marty Fletcher and Glenn Scherer.
   p. cm. — (Saving endangered species)
 Includes bibliographical references and index.
 ISBN 1-59845-033-6
 1. Green turtle—Juvenile literature. I. Scherer, Glenn. II. Title. III. Series.
 QL666.C536F58 2006
 597.92'8—dc22
                              2005015605

Printed in the United States of America

10 9 8 7 6 5 4 3 2 1

To Our Readers:
Through the purchase of this book, you and your library gain access to the Report Links that specifically
back up this book.
The Publisher will provide access to the Report Links that back up this book and will keep these Report
Links up to date on **www.myreportlinks.com** for five years from the book's first publication date.
We have done our best to make sure all Internet addresses in this book were active and appropriate when
we went to press. However, the author and the Publisher have no control over, and assume no liability
for, the material available on those Internet sites or on other Web sites they may link to.
The usage of the MyReportLinks.com Books Web site is subject to the terms and conditions stated on the
Usage Policy Statement on **www.myreportlinks.com**.
A password may be required to access the Report Links that back up this book. The password is found
on the bottom of page 4 of this book.
Any comments or suggestions can be sent by e-mail to comments@myreportlinks.com or to the address
on the back cover.

Photo Credits: © Corel Corporation, pp. 12–13, 29, 48, 71; Archie Carr National Wildlife Refuge,
p. 74; Caribbean Conservation Corporation, pp. 72, 104; CITES, p. 79; Department of Primary Industries
and Fisheries, Queensland, Australia, p. 58; Department of the Environment and Heritage, Australia,
p. 111; Earthjustice, p. 77; Enslow Publishers, Inc., pp. 5–7; Grupo Tortuguero, p. 106; Library of
Congress, p. 14; Lindsey Peavey, Grupo Tortuguero, p. 3; Marinebio.org, p. 33; MyReportLinks.com
Books, p. 4; National Geographic.com, p. 98; National Oceanographic and Atmospheric Administration
(NOAA), pp. 1, 19, 32, 35, 40, 60, 91, 92, 102, 107, 110, 112; Office of Naval Research, p. 54; PBS,
p. 97; Pro Peninsula, pp. 50, 56, 62, 87, 96, 114; Rachel Tuck, Pro Peninsula, p. 46; Sea Turtle Restoration
Project, p. 69; Seaturtle.org, p. 115; SeaWorld, p. 101; Smithsonian Institution, National Zoo, pp. 21, 37;
The Archie Carr Center for Sea Turtle Research, p. 82; The Convention on Migratory Species, p. 80; The
Marine Turtle Research Group, p. 105; The Ocean Conservancy, p. 63; Turtle Trax, pp. 9, 65, 66; United
States Fish and Wildlife Service, pp. 11, 17, 22, 26, 30–31, 42, 44–45, 75, 117; University of North
Carolina at Chapel Hill, p. 38; Watamu Turtle Watch, pp. 84, 85; World Turtle Trust, p. 53; World Wildlife
Fund, p. 88.

Cover Photo: Painet Stock Photos

CONTENTS

MyReportLinks.com Books
Great Books, Great Links, Great for Research!

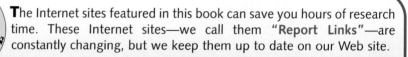

The Internet sites featured in this book can save you hours of research time. These Internet sites—we call them **"Report Links"**—are constantly changing, but we keep them up to date on our Web site.

When you see this "Approved Web Site" logo, you will know that we are directing you to a great Internet site that will help you with your research.

Give it a try! Type http://www.myreportlinks.com into your browser, click on the series title and enter the password, then click on the book title, and scroll down to the Report Links listed for this book.

The Report Links will bring you to great source documents, photographs, and illustrations. MyReportLinks.com Books save you time, feature Report Links that are kept up to date, and make report writing easier than ever! A complete listing of the Report Links can be found on pages 118–119 at the back of the book.

Please see "To Our Readers" on the copyright page for important information about this book, the MyReportLinks.com Web site, and the Report Links that back up this book.

Please enter **SGT1426** if asked for a password.

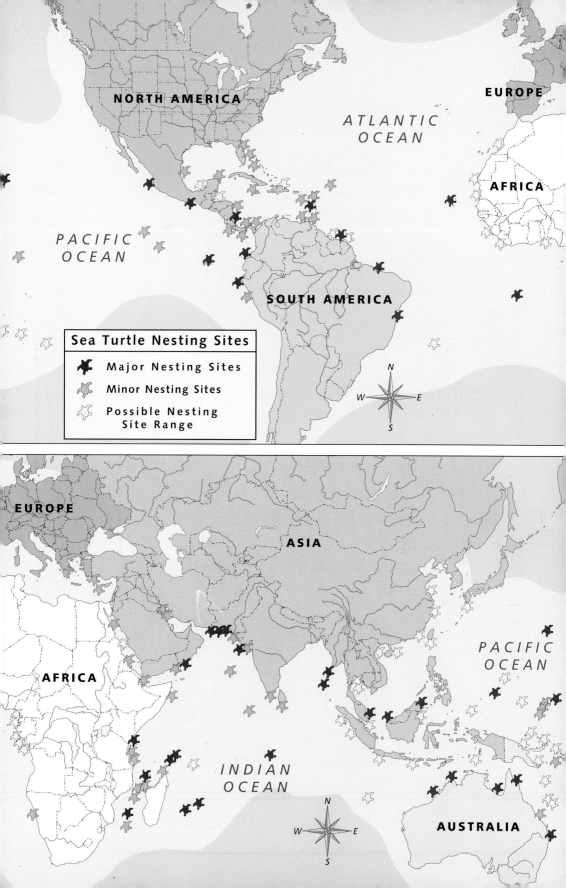

Sea Turtle Nesting Sites

★ Major Nesting Sites

★ Minor Nesting Sites

★ Possible Nesting Site Range

GREEN SEA TURTLE FACTS

▶ Scientific Name
Chelonia mydas

▶ Status
Endangered in the United States and worldwide. The green sea turtle was first listed in the United States as an endangered species in 1978.

▶ Range
Found in tropical and temperate seas worldwide including the Caribbean and Mediterranean seas; Atlantic, Pacific, and Indian oceans.

▶ Habitat
Shallow waters, in reefs, bays, and inlets, except during migration

▶ Shell Length of Adult
32 to 48 inches (81 to 122 centimeters)

▶ Weight of Adult
150 to 440 pounds (68 to 200 kilograms)

▶ Color
In adults, carapace (top part of shell) is light to dark brown with some mottling; in hatchlings, black; plastron (bottom part of shell) in adults ranges from white to light yellow to dark gray (in the Eastern Pacific green turtle); white in hatchlings. Young green sea turtles also have white margins on their limbs and their shells.

▶ Top Swimming Speed
35 miles (56.3 kilometers) per hour for short distances

▶ Deepest Diving Depth
360 feet (110 meters)

▶ Diet

Hatchlings eat both plants and animals, but adults eat mostly sea grasses and marine algae.

▶ Age at Sexual Maturity

Between 20 and 50 years

▶ Nesting Season

Varies by location. Green sea turtles nest in the Caribbean and Gulf of Mexico from March to October; in Florida from June to September; and in Hawaii from April to October.

▶ Average Number of Eggs in a Clutch

100

▶ Incubation Period

40 to 75 days, depending on nest temperatures

▶ Worldwide Population*

Based on monitoring reports from nesting beaches, researchers estimate the number of breeding females worldwide at 203,000. These numbers are stable in some areas such as Florida, Mexico, and Costa Rica, while declining in many other places. Unfortunately, in July 2005, Hurricane Emily hit one of the most important nesting areas in Mexico for green and loggerhead sea turtles and may have destroyed as many as 84,000 eggs.

▶ Major threats

Hunting of immature and adult turtles in the marine environment; killing of females and collection of eggs on nesting beaches; beach development and loss of habitat; water pollution; accidental catching and drowning by commercial fishing longlines and nets; and fibropapillomatosis (a disease that may be caused by pollution). Climate change may become a problem in this century.

The statistics on population have been compiled from several sources, including the Caribbean Conservation Corporation and Sea Turtle Survival League and the United States Fish and Wildlife Service, North Florida Field Office.

For most of the wild things on Earth, the future must depend upon the conscience of mankind.

Archie Carr

Chapter 1 ▶

THE OCEAN WORLD OF THE GREEN SEA TURTLE

Scuba diving forty feet down off the coast of Maui in the Hawaiian Islands, author Osha Gray Davidson swam with brilliantly colored tropical fish above a big boulder field. His dive partner, Ursula Keuper-Bennett, grabbed Davidson's wrist and signaled him to go deeper, pointing

A green sea turtle swims beneath Ursula Keuper-Bennett during one of her dives in Hawaii. She and her husband, Peter Bennett, are sport divers whose love of green sea turtles has led them to work toward preserving the species. Their Web site, **Turtle Trax,** offers a wealth of information about sea turtles and stunning photographs of these creatures.

EDITOR'S CHOICE

excitedly at one of the huge gray rocks on the sea floor. Davidson swam up to the smooth humped rock and inspected it. It was speckled with a few barnacles, sea creatures that attach themselves to rocks, boats, or whales. At the time he did not think it was the most interesting discovery he had ever made.

Then Davidson looked more closely at the rock and realized something startling—it was staring back at him. As he described the encounter, "In one smooth unbroken motion, the 'rock' pushes off from the ocean floor and without looking back hurls itself toward the surface. Its huge front flippers . . . sweep in slow powerful down-strokes, sending it skyward."[1] The huge "rock" had revealed itself as an adult green sea turtle!

Awestruck, Davidson looked around and realized that Ursula Keuper-Bennett had brought him to see a rare and wonderful sight: All of the "boulders" scattered around the two divers were exactly like the one that had just swum away. Davidson and his friend were surrounded by green sea turtles!

Survivors From the Age of Dinosaurs

All sea turtles are reptiles—ectothermic, or cold-blooded, egg-laying, air-breathing vertebrates, or animals with backbones. Their ancient ancestors lived on land, mostly in freshwater marshes, 200 million years ago. For some unknown reason, they moved to the salty seas about 150 million years ago.

In the ocean, they evolved into all shapes and sizes. *Archelon ischyros,* a sea turtle that lived 70 million years

▲ Sea turtles, like this green sea turtle, have existed far longer than humans, but human activity may bring about their extinction.

ago, was immense. It was the size of a small car, up to fifteen feet long. The earliest green sea turtles probably began to evolve around 50 million years ago.

Sea turtles have survived for a remarkably long time. Compare their period on Earth (150 million years) with that of humankind (5 million years)! Sea turtles have also survived against tough odds. They managed to survive the event that caused the dinosaurs to become extinct 65 million years ago. They even survived the intense cold of the ice ages that gripped the planet for much of the past 3 million years. But at the end of the fifteenth century, the green sea turtle met its greatest challenge to survival yet: modern human beings.

In 1492, Christopher Columbus made his first trip to the Americas. The Italian explorer found the Caribbean Sea so thick with sea turtles that his three ships had to halt for hours to let the migrating animals swim past. Biologists estimate that there were an astounding 60 million to 600 million green sea

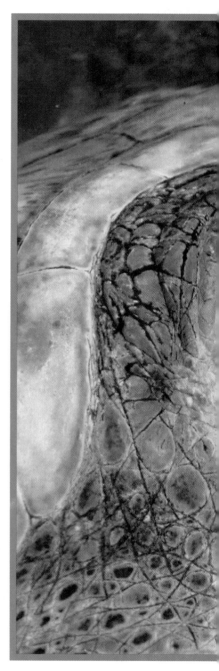

When Europeans first reached the Cayman Islands, sea turtles were abundant. Harvesting of the turtles for their meat soon led the population to be depleted. This sea turtle is one of those now protected by the Cayman Turtle Farm.

▲ This painting depicts Columbus's landing in the New World in 1492. At the time, green sea turtles were abundant in the waters of the Caribbean.

turtles living in the Caribbean before Europeans began exploring the Western Hemisphere.

While still far from the shore of one island, a member of Columbus's crew exclaimed that he could have walked to the beach on the backs of the green sea turtles in the water and never gotten wet. The turtles even saved the lives of Columbus's crew on a later voyage. After their ship was nearly wrecked by a hurricane in 1503, the starving sailors stumbled upon the Cayman Island rookery, or nesting place—probably the largest sea turtle nesting place in the entire world. The men thankfully gave up their diet of wormy bread and insects to feast on what a later explorer would describe as the green sea turtle's "very good and wholesome meate."[2]

Word spread about the bounty of turtles to be found at the Cayman Island rookery. Even a century after Columbus's voyages, an English sea captain wrote of the "infinite numbers of Sea Tortoises [that] yearly resort to lay their Eggs upon ye Sandy Bay." During the seventeenth century, great turtle fleets plundered the Cayman's beaches and waters, harvesting as many as thirteen thousand turtles each year. The green sea turtles and their eggs were fed to sailors, colonists, and slaves. One British writer declared the turtles to be an "exhaustless source of profit to the British empire."[3]

Disappearing Species

It was not true. The slaughter of the Cayman turtles greatly reduced their numbers. By the eighteenth century, the rookery collapsed, and only a few turtles were spotted even at the height of nesting season. The mariners and turtle fleets that had made such a good living harvesting green sea turtles in the Cayman Islands went elsewhere to hunt them. They then destroyed many other rookeries.

As Davidson describes the green sea turtle population in the Caribbean Sea today, "Where migrations of turtles once prevented ships from passing for hours at a time, it is a lucky sailor who today encounters more than one or two individuals while cruising the same waters. . . . The greatest assemblage of turtles the world has ever known has been methodically wiped out." Of the 60 million to 600 million green sea turtles that once swam the Caribbean, barely 60,000 adults remain.[4]

▶ Still Endangered

So it went around the globe. In much the same way that whales were hunted nearly to extinction for their oil-rich blubber during the nineteenth and twentieth centuries, green sea turtles were hunted for their meat. As recently as the 1960s, tourists in Florida could legally dine on green sea turtle steaks, burgers, and soup.

Today, even though many laws have been passed to protect the last of the green sea turtles, they are still highly endangered. Adult turtles and their eggs are still legally hunted for food in many nations, while other serious human-caused dangers threaten the animals. Commercial shrimp fishermen accidentally catch turtles in their nets and drown them. Plastic trash and oil spills have a negative impact on the turtles, while coastal development destroys their nesting beaches. And now a mysterious disease that produces large tumors plagues green sea turtles. Of the many millions of green sea turtles that once swam the world's oceans, only 203,000 adult females are believed to remain, although it is difficult to come up with an accurate estimate since not all nesting sites are monitored. Even that number is thought to be diminishing, not growing.

There is still hope for green sea turtles. That hope bloomed in 1970, when 3 million Americans marched in the streets on the first-ever Earth Day. It was the biggest public march and demonstration in United States history,

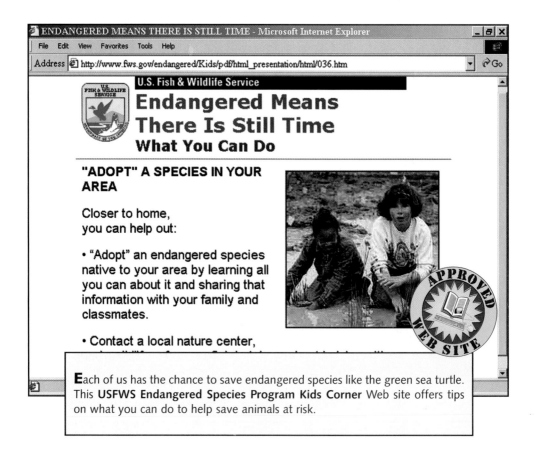

Each of us has the chance to save endangered species like the green sea turtle. This **USFWS Endangered Species Program Kids Corner** Web site offers tips on what you can do to help save animals at risk.

and it has inspired thousands of people to try to save the world's most endangered wildlife ever since. Among those rare and endangered animals is the green sea turtle.

To the Rescue: You Can Help Save This Species!

It is easy for young people to get involved in saving green sea turtles. For those who live or vacation at the ocean or along any river or stream that feeds into the sea, a simple first step is to put on a pair of gloves and begin picking up litter on the beach or along the shore.

Plastic bags, Styrofoam drinking cups, six-pack plastic rings, tangles of nylon fishing line, and other synthetic materials can harm green sea turtles. Even cigarette butts can be deadly to them. Turtles mistake this trash for food, and when they eat it, their digestive systems can become clogged. Fishing line can wrap around turtles' necks, suffocating them, or around the turtle flippers, cutting off blood circulation.

That is why it is important to wash and reuse plastic bags rather than tossing them away after just one use. You can also get involved in local recycling programs, making sure that plastics, cans, and bottles get to recycling centers and that used motor oil and old batteries are disposed of properly through hazardous waste programs. None of these things has to wind up in our oceans, polluting them, unless we treat the oceans as a huge trash receptacle. That means not pouring harmful chemicals down sinks or merely tossing them in a storm drain, because they will wind up in the oceans, eventually.

▲ *This sea turtle died unnecessarily after becoming entangled in a gill net.*

▷ Join an Organization

One of the easiest ways for you to get involved in saving green sea turtles is through an environmental group like the Caribbean Conservation Corporation and Sea Turtle Survival League. The best way, however, to help save green sea turtles is through education: Learn as much as you can about them. By learning about their life cycle, about their value to people and to the world's oceans, and about what threatens them, you can become an ambassador for the species, teaching others about this endangered reptile.

Education Is Key

You can educate your family, friends, and classmates and get them to team up with you to spring into action by cleaning beaches or collecting donations for nonprofit groups that are working to protect sea turtles. Other actions might involve writing letters via e-mail and regular mail to government officials who are in a position to help save turtles by making laws. You might even make saving sea turtles a career! As renowned sea turtle scientist and activist James R. Spotila suggests, "If you are a student and care about the future of sea turtles you should study to be a biologist or conservationist."[5]

Why Save Sea Turtles?

One of the questions you might get asked by people you talk to about green sea turtles is, Why is it important to save them? In other words, why should we care?

First of all, if humans cause sea turtles to go extinct, we will have killed off one of the most ancient animals on the planet. Sea turtles come from a line of creatures that appeared 145 million years before our first human ancestor walked the earth! Such a loss would be devastating to scientists who want to learn more not only about green sea turtles themselves but also about how animal species have evolved since the days of the dinosaurs.

Green sea turtles are also stunning creatures that inspire people with their beauty and grace. Their loss would make the world a less beautiful, less wild, and less wonderful place to live in.

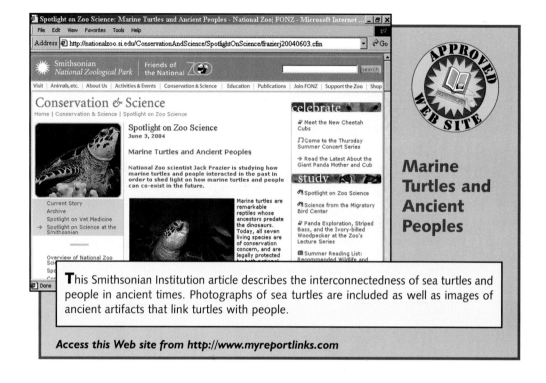

This Smithsonian Institution article describes the interconnectedness of sea turtles and people in ancient times. Photographs of sea turtles are included as well as images of ancient artifacts that link turtles with people.

Access this Web site from http://www.myreportlinks.com

On a more practical note, ecologists recognize that every creature has its special place in its ecosystem, the community of plants and animals that forms an environment. When a species goes extinct, its disappearance affects the natural balance within an ecosystem in which species depend on each other. It may even cause other organisms to fail. Green sea turtles, for example, graze on algae, simple plants found in or near water. Without the turtles, the algae can grow out of control, smothering coral reefs and endangering other animals such as fish and shellfish. Too much algae can cause an entire coral reef ecosystem to collapse.

▲ *When we allow our beaches to become dumping grounds, we hurt ourselves as well as all marine wildlife.*

There is a final good reason to save sea turtles, and it is a selfish one. Researchers are alarmed at how quickly our oceans are being polluted and overfished. In this century, the world's oceans could become nearly barren of life, leaving millions of people without their primary source of food. To protect endangered species like green sea turtles, we also must protect the oceans in which they live. By doing that, we protect our global seafood supply. If we end ocean pollution in order to save green sea turtles, we will also be making the seas safer for every animal that lives there. And that will improve commercial fishing.

If we remove trash from our beaches to protect sea turtles, those beaches will become safer for all wildlife and more enjoyable for people, too. So everything we do to save green sea turtles and other endangered species benefits all creatures—including us.

ALL ABOUT SEA TURTLES

Sea turtles have mystified human beings for centuries. People living by the coast on five continents have watched these large beasts drag themselves out of the waves onto beaches. They have watched these massive turtles lumber through the sand, laboriously dig a shallow hole with their flippers, lay and bury their eggs, and then disappear back into the deep.

Some people have had the good luck to see these seemingly clumsy creatures under water. There they become graceful swimmers, gliding effortlessly above a Caribbean sandy sea bottom or coral reef or through a Pacific kelp forest.

▶ The Seven Species of Sea Turtles

Green sea turtles are not the only turtles to inhabit the oceans. They share the water with six other species of sea turtles: Kemp's Ridley, olive Ridley, flatback, hawksbill, loggerhead, and leatherback. The olive Ridley and loggerhead are listed as threatened while the other five species are listed as endangered under the United States Endangered Species Act. Florida and Eastern Pacific green sea turtles are considered endangered.

This fisherman (inset) on a Texas beach holds up a Kemp's Ridley sea turtle that he accidentally caught and then freed. After carefully setting the turtle down, the fisherman, a conservationist committed to preserving the sea and its wildlife, watched it swim away.

The Kemp's Ridley

The Kemp's Ridley sea turtle *(Lepidochelys kempii)* is among the smallest of sea turtles, with a shell length of 24 to 30 inches (61 to 76 centimeters). It is also among the most endangered and nests only in the Gulf of Mexico. In his book *Wildlife in America,* author Peter Matthiessen wrote about their decline: "In the late 1940s, a photographer filmed . . . some forty thousand Ridleys coming ashore on the beach at Rancho Nuevo in Mexico. In 1985, in the course of the entire season, only 518 females nested at Rancho Nuevo, the only known nesting beach of real significance for the entire species."[1] The Kemp's Ridley has recovered slightly since then, with more than five thousand breeding females thought to be alive today. Biologists remain cautiously hopeful that this sea turtle can be saved.

The Olive Ridley

The olive Ridley sea turtle *(Lepidochelys olivacea)* is about the same size as the Kemp's Ridley. It is the most abundant sea turtle and ranges over the tropical Pacific, Indian, and Atlantic oceans. Although there are an estimated 4 million adult olive ridleys, they too are in serious and quick decline. As recently as 1950, there were 10 million olive Ridleys in Mexico alone. Olive Ridleys are also found off the coast of Thailand in Asia and Suriname in South America. But off the Orissa Peninsula in India, thousands of olive Ridleys are being killed each year through incidental bycatch (accidental catch) in shrimp trawler nets. If numbers continue to plummet, olive Ridleys could be in big trouble.

The Flatback

Flatback sea turtles *(Natator depressus)* are larger than the two Ridleys. They nest only on beaches in Australia and are considered the most mysterious of sea turtles. Little is known about what this species eats or the path of its migration from nesting to foraging grounds. There are about thirty thousand mature females alive today, and the Australian government is doing a good job of protecting its nesting beaches. But the fact that the flatback lives in only one part of the ocean, rather than being spread around the globe, could make it more vulnerable to extinction.

The Hawksbill

The hawksbill turtle *(Eretmochelys imbricata)* is much larger than the Ridleys but slightly smaller than the flatback. It has the misfortune of having a beautiful shell marked by bright rays of yellow, white, red, black, brown, and gold. The shell material, known in many cultures as tortoiseshell, is so beautiful that it has been harvested by everyone from the Egyptians to the Romans, ancient Chinese, Arabs, and American Indians to make fine jewelry, combs, and furniture inlays. Thankfully, plastic imitations of tortoiseshell have largely replaced the real thing. Hawksbill turtles are found worldwide, nesting in eighty-two nations. There are

The beauty of the hawksbill's shell is, unfortunately, the reason why hawksbills were harvested for hundreds of years.

probably only about seventy-eight thousand nesting females left.

The Loggerhead

The loggerhead sea turtle (*Caretta caretta*) is larger than all the other species named so far, with a shell length of 34 to 49 inches (86 to 124 centimeters). It has a large crushing jaw so it can feed on large hard-bodied prey items such as big shellfish or crustaceans. Loggerheads are doing fairly well in the western Atlantic, while their population remains stable in the Mediterranean.

While green sea turtles arc known for being gentle, loggerheads have been known to turn nasty when disturbed. In 1905, a story in the *New York Herald* told of five men in a rowboat who tried to catch a 610-pound (277-kilogram) loggerhead. The angry turtle fought

▲ *This female loggerhead at the Archie Carr National Wildlife Refuge in Florida returns to the sea after laying her eggs on the beach. The tracking device on her back allows researchers to monitor her movements.*

capture by using its flippers to nearly turn the boat on its side. It also chewed the oars and tore at one man's arm. The turtle then swam away, according to Archie Carr in his *Handbook of Turtles*.[2] Carr was a conservation biologist whose pioneering work with sea turtles led him to become known as the "father of turtle research."

The Leatherback

The leatherback sea turtle *(Dermochelys coriacea)* is the largest of the sea turtles, 52 to 70 inches (132 to 178 centimeters) long. It can weigh up to a ton (907 kilograms). It lacks a hard shell, but instead has a rubbery skin strengthened by thousands of tiny bone plates. Leatherbacks may have inspired the legends told by sailors about sea serpents. Unfortunately, this turtle sometimes mistakes discarded plastic bags floating in the sea

for jellyfish, one of its favorite foods. And other species of sea turtles regularly make the same mistake. Plastic does a great deal of harm to turtles, cutting their skin and sometimes choking them.[3] There may be fewer than fifty thousand nesting female leatherbacks left, and they are among the most endangered sea turtles. Although the number of leatherbacks in the Atlantic is increasing,

▲ This leatherback sea turtle takes a rest on a sandy beach at the Canaveral National Seashore, Florida. Leatherbacks are the largest sea turtles.

the Pacific leatherback, some researchers fear, may go extinct in that region within the next twenty years.

▶ The Green Sea Turtle

The seventh sea turtle species is the green sea turtle. Its scientific name is *Chelonia mydas,* which literally means "turtle from the sea." It is probably the best known sea turtle to Americans since it can be found in the east in the waters along all Gulf coast states, north to Long Island Sound, and south to the U.S. Virgin Islands and Puerto Rico, and in the west off California and Hawaii.

It is known for its grace in the water, its beautiful shell, and its big gentle eyes. Unfortunately, humans have also long found it utterly delicious. The animal's green fat (made that color by a steady vegetarian diet of algae and sea grass) and muscle can be cooked into the tastiest of turtle soups and also as steaks. For that and many other reasons, the green sea turtle is endangered.

A Beautiful Swimmer

Sea turtle expert James Spotila offers a wonderful description of the green sea turtle: "It is everything one would expect to see in such a creature. Large, with a

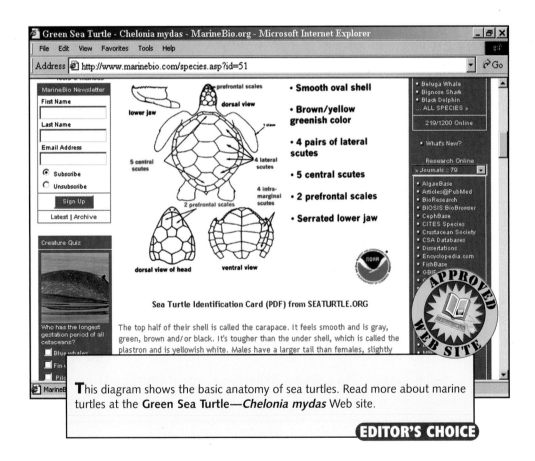

This diagram shows the basic anatomy of sea turtles. Read more about marine turtles at the **Green Sea Turtle—*Chelonia mydas*** Web site.

EDITOR'S CHOICE

distinguished, inquisitive face, it flies through the water with ease. Its shell is nicely rounded and gives off a brilliant sheen in the water . . . Its well-formed flippers . . . appear a bit small for its body size but are quite efficient for propelling it through the oceans."[4] The turtle uses its flippers much like a bird's wings, soaring and diving through the water.

The green sea turtle gets its name from the green color of the fat and muscle under its shell. Its head is small, but unlike some land turtles, it cannot pull its head inside its shell. It sees well under water, but is nearsighted on land. It has no teeth, but its jaws are serrated like a jagged knife so that they can tear tough sea grasses. The top portion of its shell, called the carapace, is smooth and has large plates, called scutes. These scutes are made of keratin, a tough but lightweight protein substance that is like human fingernails.

▷ Turtle Shells

The carapace color varies from pale to dark green, brown, or even black. The plastron, the part of the shell that covers the turtle's belly, is whitish or yellowish in Atlantic and Hawaiian green sea turtles and dark graygreen in Eastern Pacific green sea turtles.

The shells of adults are from 32 to 48 inches (80 to 122 centimeters) long, and adult green sea turtles weigh from 150 to 440 pounds (68 to 200 kilograms). But they can be much larger: The largest green sea turtle on record was 5 feet (1.5 meters) long and weighed 871 pounds (395 kilograms).[5]

▲ *Sea grass provides sea turtles with much of their diet.*

Green sea turtle carapaces can be covered with patches of algae, which fishes feed on. This partnership between fish and turtle is an example of what scientists call symbiosis, a relationship between two different species that benefits them both over a long period of time. In this case, the fish gets a free meal, and the green sea turtle gets a clean shell.

Adults eat mostly sea grasses (especially one favorite type called turtle grass) and algae that grow in shallow waters. Adult green turtles are the only sea turtles that are herbivorous, or vegetarian, eating mostly plants. They like to graze on the youngest shoots of sea grass because they are the most tender and because they have the highest protein value.

Sea turtles grow very slowly, not reaching sexual maturity (the age at which they can mate) until they are twenty to fifty years of age. This slow growth is caused by their vegetarian diet. Meat contains a lot of protein and allows for quicker growth. Sea grass, even the tender new shoots, has far less protein than meat.

The very long time that it takes green sea turtles to reach sexual maturity is one reason the species is endangered. Many juvenile green sea turtles, sickened by pollution or drowned in fishing nets, never reach maturity and never mate or lay eggs.

▶ Citizens of the World

Green sea turtles are found in all of the temperate and tropical waters throughout the world. They can be found in the coastal waters of 140 nations. In the Western Hemisphere, they can be seen as far north as Massachusetts and Alaska and as far south as southern Brazil and Chile.

They have major nesting sites in eighty countries. They nest primarily in the Gulf of Mexico and Caribbean Sea; along the coasts of Central and South America; in Hawaii, Australia, and Indonesia; in many places in the Indian Ocean including along Madagascar and Saudi Arabia; and throughout the eastern Mediterranean Sea.

Major United States nesting sites are on Florida's southeastern coast. In 2004, the Florida Fish and Wildlife Conservation Commission's Fish and Wildlife Research Institute, which coordinates sea turtle monitoring programs, counted 3,577 green sea turtle nests statewide.[6]

http://photo2.si.edu/turtles/11959.gif - Microsoft Internet Explorer

File   Edit   View   Favorites   Tools   Help

Address | http://photo2.si.edu/turtles/11959.gif

A photographer for the Smithsonian Institution captured this view of the beach at Tortuguero National Park, in Costa Rica, a major nesting place for green sea turtles. Learn more about her trip to photograph **Nesting Sea Turtles** at this Web site.

In the Hawaiian Islands, 580 nesting females are seen annually, with the remote French Frigate Shoals being their largest nesting site. Green sea turtles in Hawaii are rather isolated, and they do not appear to ever mix with other populations of green sea turtles in the Pacific. They stay almost exclusively in Hawaiian waters.

The Largest Nesting Group

The largest nesting colony of green sea turtles in the Western Hemisphere is found on the black sand beaches of Tortuguero, Costa Rica, where about 23,000 females come to nest each year. (*Tortuguero* is Spanish for "region

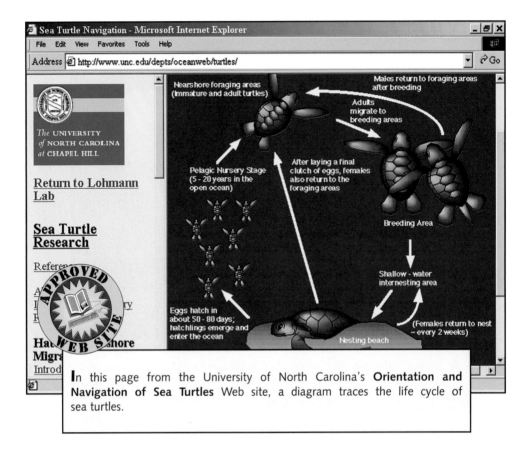

Sea Turtle Navigation - Microsoft Internet Explorer

File   Edit   View   Favorites   Tools   Help

Address http://www.unc.edu/depts/oceanweb/turtles/

The UNIVERSITY
of NORTH CAROLINA
at CHAPEL HILL

Return to Lohmann Lab

Sea Turtle Research

Nearshore foraging areas (Immature and adult turtles)

Males return to foraging areas after breeding

Adults migrate to breeding areas

Pelagic Nursery Stage (5 - 20 years in the open ocean)

After laying a final clutch of eggs, females also return to the foraging areas

Breeding Area

Shallow - water internesting area

Eggs hatch in about 50 - 80 days; hatchlings emerge and enter the ocean

(Females return to nest ~ every 2 weeks)

Nesting beach

In this page from the University of North Carolina's **Orientation and Navigation of Sea Turtles** Web site, a diagram traces the life cycle of sea turtles.

of turtles.") The largest colony in the world is found on Raine Island, in Australia's Great Barrier Reef, where during peak nesting years, thousands nest nightly. When not mating, green sea turtles spend most of their time in shallow water. They live near coastlines and around islands, near coral reefs, in rocky and sandy areas where algae and sea grasses, their choice foods, are plentiful.

Though they spend most of their time in shallow water, green sea turtles are excellent divers and can descend 360 feet (110 meters) under water. Researchers are not sure how long green sea turtles stay submerged, on average, before needing to come to the surface to get another breath of air. Some green sea turtles have been known to stay under water for a maximum of sixty-six minutes, a record beaten among all seven sea turtle species only by the hawksbill turtle, which can stay submerged for seventy-four minutes. Compare this with the average human being's ability to stay under water just two and a half minutes![7]

The Beginning of Life

Life begins for a new green sea turtle when an adult female awkwardly drags herself ashore at night onto a nesting beach. Remarkably, the female nests on the exact same beach where she was born many years earlier. She digs a hole in the sand and lays a clutch that averages about one hundred eggs.

Archie Carr describes this process beautifully:

> Everybody ought to see a turtle nesting. It is an impressive thing to see, the pilgrimage of a sea creature back to the land its ancestors left a hundred million years ago. The nesting rites begin, for the watcher, at least, when the turtle strands in the surf. . . . The turtle is wild and skittish when she first touches shore, and even the light of a match struck far up the beach may send her back to the sea. . . . In strong moonlight you can make the turtle out. . . . You can see her stop with the backwash foaming flame around her, push her head this way and that with a darting motion less like the slow movement you expect of a green turtle than like a lizard or snake, then lower her head and nose the hard, wet beach as if to smell for telltale signs of generations of ancestors there before her.[8]

Once ashore, the female turtle climbs the beach, looking for an ideal dry spot to lay her eggs, usually where

▲ Researchers investigate the eggs in a green sea turtle's nest on Helen's Reef, in Western Caroline Islands, in the Pacific.

beach plants begin or beside a sand dune or log. Once she starts digging a hole with her flippers, she becomes totally focused on her task. Carr describes the scene: "If a turtle is really of a mind to lay, she can be watched . . . by gangs of people waving flashlights in her face, and will go on through her set maneuvers oblivious to any amount of hullabaloo."[9]

With the golf-ball–sized eggs safely dropped in the neatly prepared pit, the turtle throws sand over them by tossing it in the air with her flippers. The sand hides the location of the eggs from predator animals that might eat them. The female then drags her body back to the sea, vanishing into the night waves.

Female green turtles may lay from one to seven clutches of eggs in each nesting season, spending about two weeks at sea between trips to the beach to lay a clutch of eggs, which averages 100 eggs. The time of year when the nesting season happens varies at different locations around the world. Females rarely nest every year and may wait as long as six years before mating and nesting again, but nesting more often happens at two-, three-, and four-year intervals.

From Egg to Hatchling

The eggs are not hard-shelled like chicken eggs but are softer and leathery feeling. They incubate in the sun-warmed sand for forty to seventy-two days. Amazingly, the temperature of the hot sand will determine whether a baby turtle will be male or female. The hotter the sand, the more eggs will become females. The cooler the sand, the more will become males.

If the eggs are undisturbed, more than 90 percent will hatch. The babies, called hatchlings, weigh less than one ounce (28 grams) at birth and are about two inches (five centimeters) long. Their carapaces are black, their plastrons, white, and their limbs and shells also have white margins.

The entire clutch of one hundred or so eggs hatches at about the same time two feet under the sand in the safety of the nest. Once they leave the egg, the young turtles spend up to forty-eight hours underground

A sign in the sand at Florida's Hobe Sound National Wildlife Refuge warns beachgoers to tread carefully—the protected area is a sea turtle nesting beach from May to October.

absorbing their egg-yolk sacs. Then they begin to struggle toward the surface of the beach.

Their bursting out of the sand from the nest was described in 1555 by Peter Martyr in his book *The Decades of the Newe Worlde.* He wrote: "At the daye appoynted of nature to the procreation of these beautes, there escapeth owte a multitude of tortoyles . . . [as if they were] swarming owte of an ante hyll."[10]

At this moment, the hatchlings are most vulnerable to predators prowling the beach. Fortunately, nature has provided these tiny creatures with some protection. If hatchlings climb from the nest toward the beach surface on a sunny day, they get too hot and stop moving. When things cool down in the evening, they start to move again. As a result, almost all green sea turtles leave their nests under the cover and safety of darkness, though some are still snatched up by raccoons, night herons, and other animals. At rare times, cool cloudy days fool the hatchlings into thinking it is nighttime, and they reach the beach surface during the daylight. That makes them easy targets for sharp-eyed predators.

Some predators such as dogs have a keen sense of smell and can detect hatchlings from a great distance. In Costa Rica, it is not unusual for dogs to arrive at sea turtle nests just at the moment the hatchlings come bubbling out of them.

Life in the Sea

After the hatchlings scramble on their flippers quickly into the sea, these tiny omnivores feed on almost anything

Even though green sea turtles are the largest hard-shelled sea turtles, they still face many threats.

▲ *A green sea turtle swimming off Kauai, Hawaii. Green sea turtles migrate incredible distances to reach their nesting grounds.*

they can scrounge up, including algae, plankton, small jellyfish, shrimp, fish eggs, worms, insects, and snails. The addition of meat to their diets gives them extra protein to grow faster.

Green sea turtles do not become herbivores, eating only algae and sea grasses (though maybe an occasional jellyfish), until later in life when their shells are 8 to 10 inches (20 to 25 centimeters) long. From that time onward, their growth is much slower.

Being a green sea turtle is not easy, even without the many threats posed by human beings. Hungry ghost crabs, birds, dogs, cats, raccoons, coyotes, and other land predators snatch many of the hatchlings up before they can complete their race to the sea. Ocean predators such as fish, pelicans, gulls, and terns eat more baby turtles before they get very big. It is estimated that less than half the hatchlings survive their first year. Even adult turtles are not safe. Sharks, most commonly tiger sharks, sometimes eat them. Though no one knows for sure, it is believed that less than one percent of all hatchlings live long enough to reproduce.

Great Ocean Travelers

In their earliest years, hatchlings swim quite a lot but are mostly swept about by sea currents in the open ocean. Eventually, as they become strong swimmers, they find their way to feeding grounds in the shallow coves, bays, and lagoons of protected islands and coasts. For a long time it was thought that green sea turtles never left the water except to nest. But in remote parts of the world not populated by people, green sea turtles have been discovered on beaches in the daytime, basking in the sun. They may do this to warm their bodies, to be safe from tiger sharks, or to dry their shells in order to kill algae growing on them.

The juvenile turtles probably do not travel too far from their feeding ground until they reach sexual maturity at age twenty to fifty, although they may visit a few different foraging areas. Then they migrate, somehow homing in on the beach where they were born. Once there, the males and females go to a courtship area just off shore near the nesting beach. There they mate.

A sandy beach on the Galápagos Islands is marked by the tracks of a green sea turtle. Chelonia mydas is the only sea turtle species that actually nests on these Pacific islands, which lie six hundred miles off Ecuador's coast.

Green sea turtles often migrate long distances from their foraging grounds to nesting grounds. For example, some shuttle regularly between feeding grounds off the coast of Brazil, all the way to nesting beaches on Ascension Island in the middle of the Atlantic Ocean, more than 1,240 miles (2,000 kilometers) away.

The Mystery of Migration

Since there is only open ocean in between and no landmarks, scientists have long wondered how the turtles find their way. Some researchers are convinced that sea turtles could only make such long-distance trips if they had miniature magnetic "compasses" in their brains to help them find their way. However, when researchers recently strapped powerful magnets to green sea turtles to disrupt any magnetic compass they might have in their heads, the researchers were surprised. The big magnets did not throw off the turtle's aim at all, and they were still able to safely complete their migration between Ascension Island and Brazil. The scientists point out that this does not mean that the turtles have no such compass—it only means that whatever mechanism guides their navigation is still unidentified. They think that the turtles may use their memories, the position of the sun and stars, or chemical concentrations in ocean water to find their way. It will take more research to find out exactly how green sea turtles can pinpoint their ancestral nesting beaches.[11]

Oddly enough, turtles that forage near perfect nesting beaches typically do not lay their eggs on those beaches.

This Eastern Pacific green sea turtle has been radio-tagged by researchers so its movements can be tracked in San Diego Bay.

Instead, the turtles migrate great distances back to where they were born, to a beach known as their natal beach.

After the nesting season, males and females migrate back to their foraging grounds. There the female will feed on sea grass or marine algae until she is ready to mate again, which may be as long as four years after her last breeding period. The reason it takes so long to mate again is that the female needs to build up a lot of fat for the work that lies ahead. She needs enough energy to swim the migration route and produce up to eight hundred eggs for the seven clutches to be laid in a breeding season.

Green Sea Turtle Life Span

Researchers do not know how long green sea turtles live because the turtles spend most of their lives hidden in the sea, and there is not a reliable method for examining them and determining their exact ages. But some scientists believe that these turtles can outlive the average human being, whose life span is about seventy-eight years. Some researchers think that the age of a sea turtle can be determined by the annual "growth" rings formed by the turtle's bones, since in almost all reptiles, new bone grows on the outside of old bone, in cycles, that produces distinct layers.[12]

Now that human pressures are so intense on green sea turtles, it seems likely that the animals are not living as long today as they once lived under more natural and less difficult conditions.

Chapter 3

THREATS TO GREEN SEA TURTLES

There were once many millions of green sea turtles worldwide, but as the human population grew and spread out over the earth, the turtles' numbers began to drop. Today, there are probably fewer than a quarter of a million nesting green sea turtles, although it is very difficult to estimate the size of that population. The number

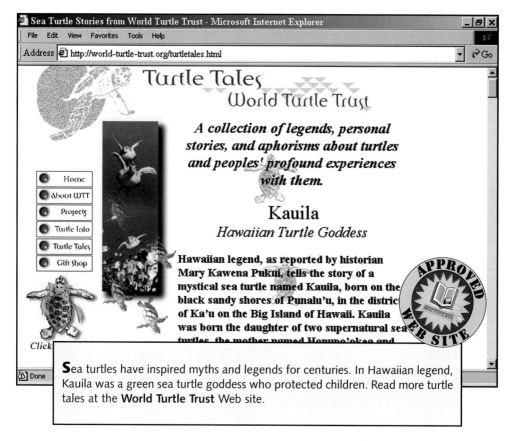

Sea turtles have inspired myths and legends for centuries. In Hawaiian legend, Kauila was a green sea turtle goddess who protected children. Read more turtle tales at the **World Turtle Trust** Web site.

of juvenile male and female turtles and the number of adult male green sea turtles is larger, but exact numbers are not known.

Green sea turtles have been harvested since ancient times. People have killed them for their meat and eggs and have used their carapaces for art and decoration. The six-thousand-year-old bones of sea turtles have been found in what was once ancient Mesopotamia (now Iraq). The Mesopotamian god of waters, Enki, was often represented as a turtle. Ancient Greek coins were also adorned with turtle images. In fact, the green sea turtle's scientific name, *Chelonia mydas,* was coined by the ancient Greek philosopher Aristotle. The name stuck and has been in use for twenty-three-hundred years.

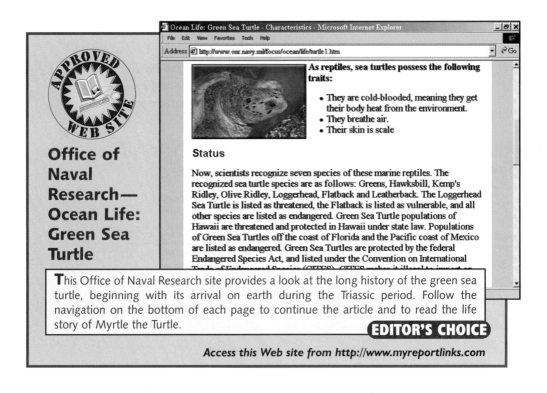

Office of Naval Research— Ocean Life: Green Sea Turtle

Ocean Life: Green Sea Turtle - Characteristics - Microsoft Internet Explorer

File   Edit   View   Favorites   Tools   Help

Address http://www.onr.navy.mil/focus/ocean/life/turtle1.htm

As reptiles, sea turtles possess the following traits:

- They are cold-blooded, meaning they get their body heat from the environment.
- They breathe air.
- Their skin is scale

Status

Now, scientists recognize seven species of these marine reptiles. The recognized sea turtle species are as follows: Greens, Hawksbill, Kemp's Ridley, Olive Ridley, Loggerhead, Flatback and Leatherback. The Loggerhead Sea Turtle is listed as threatened, the Flatback is listed as vulnerable, and all other species are listed as endangered. Green Sea Turtle populations of Hawaii are threatened and protected in Hawaii under state law. Populations of Green Sea Turtles off the coast of Florida and the Pacific coast of Mexico are listed as endangered. Green Sea Turtles are protected by the federal Endangered Species Act, and listed under the Convention on International

This Office of Naval Research site provides a look at the long history of the green sea turtle, beginning with its arrival on earth during the Triassic period. Follow the navigation on the bottom of each page to continue the article and to read the life story of Myrtle the Turtle.

EDITOR'S CHOICE

Access this Web site from http://www.myreportlinks.com

In ancient Hindu mythology, the world rested atop four elephants that stood upon the carapace of an immense sea turtle. In Hawaii, folk legends tell of a young green sea turtle goddess named Kauila who could take the form of a young girl to watch over Hawaiian children playing on the beach.

Scientists thought that the harvesting of sea turtles by people in ancient times did little damage to ocean ecosystems. But a 2001 study found that overfishing by early peoples may have been the first step in damaging ocean habitats. "Ecosystem collapse was set in motion long before modern activities contributed," says marine ecologist Karen Bjorndal.[1] She found that American Indians harvesting too many green sea turtles had a negative impact not only on local coastal ecosystems where the turtles nest but also over the much wider region where they live and feed.

Modern Curiosity

In the twentieth century, people who had never seen green sea turtles looked upon them with great curiosity, if not with respect. In the 1930s, on a small island off the coast of Australia, visitors ran a "turtle derby." A writer for *National Geographic* magazine described the scene as tourists climbed atop the shells of basking green turtles: "Thus surprised, [the turtles] scrambled over the sand, plowing quaint furrows with their flippers. . . . Once in fairly deep water, the turtle won the game. A dive unseated the rider, who splashed ashore for another little joyride to the sea."[2]

Unfortunately, as annoying as a "turtle derby" might have been to the green sea turtle so rudely awakened, people have done far worse things to sea turtles. Most of the major threats to this species come from modern people and technologies.

Turtle Hunting

The same 1930s *National Geographic* article that reported the playful "turtle derby" also reported on a nearby turtle-soup factory that produced 36,000 tins of soup, which represented about 1,000 turtles harvested in a typical season.[3]

Easy to catch on land or in water and easy to keep alive for long periods of time in pens, green sea turtles were a popular food source for the colonists of the New World. Turtle flesh and fat was carved into steaks or became the key ingredient of green turtle soup. Hungry sailors and fishermen sailing the globe fed on green sea turtles. Until laws were passed late in the twentieth century, the species was proudly served on the tables of many of the world's leading restaurants including those in the United States. Wealthy people in places like New York and London raved about turtle

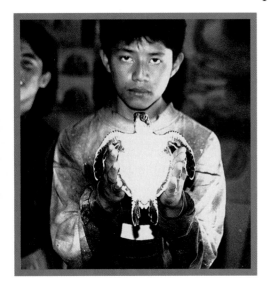

◁ *A young boy in Michoacán holds a juvenile Eastern Pacific green sea turtle. Sea turtles, once hunted in great numbers in Mexico, are now protected there.*

meat and turtle soup as a delicacy. This high demand caused poor people to overharvest green sea turtle nesting beaches and foraging areas to make the money they needed to feed their families.

Hunting continues to take a heavy toll on green sea turtles today. In the Mexican state of Michoacán, hunting was largely responsible for reducing a green sea turtle nesting colony from 25,000 adult females in the 1970s to about 2,000 today. One village in Baja California hunted 200 turtles a week, with so many being eaten that the turtles were nicknamed the Gulf of California's "black steer."[4]

Though it has been on the federal list of endangered species since 1978, the green sea turtle is still on the menu in other countries. Almost every part of the turtle's body is harvested, processed, and bought and sold, both legally and illegally. Turtle meat and eggs are still eaten, their fat is still used as oil, their skin continues to be made into small leather goods, and their shells continue to be crafted into jewelry and ornaments. Unfortunately, the rarer green sea turtles become, the more valuable they will be to hunters harvesting them.

Death by Accident

One significant threat to green sea turtles is unintended capture and killing by commercial fishing fleets around the world. Many turtles die accidentally when they are caught up in fishing gear that includes nets and lines.

Commercial shrimp fishers use large trawler nets that are dragged behind their boats. These nets trap and drown more than ten thousand sea turtles each year. Many of

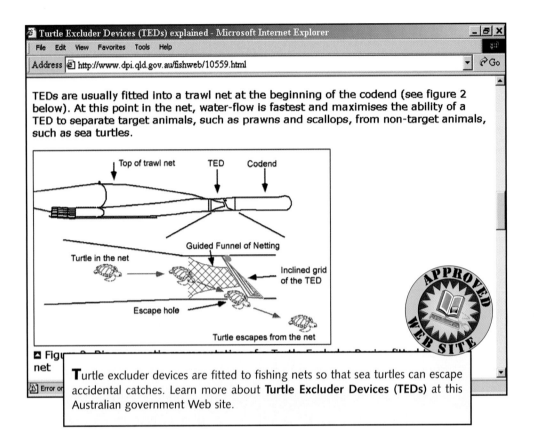

Turtle Excluder Devices (TEDs) explained - Microsoft Internet Explorer

File   Edit   View   Favorites   Tools   Help

Address http://www.dpi.qld.gov.au/fishweb/10559.html

TEDs are usually fitted into a trawl net at the beginning of the codend (see figure 2 below). At this point in the net, water-flow is fastest and maximises the ability of a TED to separate target animals, such as prawns and scallops, from non-target animals, such as sea turtles.

Top of trawl net   TED   Codend

Guided Funnel of Netting

Turtle in the net

Inclined grid of the TED

Escape hole

Turtle escapes from the net

Turtle excluder devices are fitted to fishing nets so that sea turtles can escape accidental catches. Learn more about **Turtle Excluder Devices (TEDs)** at this Australian government Web site.

these turtles could be saved if shrimpers would use turtle excluder devices, called TEDs, that keep turtles out of the shrimp nets. Unfortunately, TEDs are not perfect, and some turtles caught inside TED-equipped trawler nets die anyway. Though laws require the use of TEDs in United States waters, and most shrimpers use them, some do not because they believe that the device cuts down on their shrimp harvest and therefore on their profits.

Turtles are also accidentally caught up and drowned by other types of fishing gear. Gill nets, also called drift nets, are immense nets set adrift by fishing boats.

Nicknamed "walls of death," these nets float through the ocean, capturing fish by the thousands. Unfortunately, they also entangle sea turtles, killing them. The biggest open ocean drift nets, which are many miles long, have been banned. But many conservationists believe that some ships equipped with giant drift nets still illegally sail the high seas, poaching fish and killing turtles.

Longlines are another serious problem, especially in the Pacific Ocean. These are baited fishing lines with thousands of hooks that stretch for miles under the sea. Though the hooks are meant to catch tuna and sword-fish, they often catch and drown turtles instead.

Sometimes, these lines and nets continue to catch and kill fish and turtles even when they are no longer used for fishing—these "ghost nets" float abandoned in the sea after they have been lost or discarded by fishing boats.

▷ Coastal Development

Adult green sea turtles always return to the same beach to mate and lay their eggs. But they cannot return if the beach where they were born no longer exists. Human development around the world is destroying pristine nesting beaches, replacing them with cities, towns, ship ports, resorts, marinas, and docks. That leaves the turtles with no place to lay their eggs.

Even if the beach itself is not destroyed, beachside activity can still cause big problems. Noise and lights can disturb female nesting turtles, and beach obstructions such as jetties and bulkheads can keep hatchlings from reaching the ocean. Some beach communities use large

▲ Longlines are fishing lines that stretch for long distances in the ocean. Unfortunately, sea turtles are sometimes their unintentional catch.

mechanized rakes to smooth out their beach sand, which can disturb or even destroy turtle nests.

Off-road vehicles traveling along beaches can also disturb nesting turtles. These vehicles compact the sand, making it difficult for females to dig nests. They can also destroy the nests after the eggs are laid. Deep tire ruts left by such vehicles block the tiny hatchlings from reaching the sea. Recreational motor boaters sometimes collide with adult turtles, gashing their bodies with the boats' propellers.

Dredging, the deepening of ship or boating channels, can disturb turtles too. So can beach replenishment. This is a process in which offshore sand is pumped onto a beach or trucked in to make the beach larger after storms have washed parts of it away. Beach replenishment is a problem for turtles because this new sand may heat up too much or pack differently than the natural beach, making poor nests.

A change in beach vegetation can also harm green sea turtles. Trees or other nonnative beach vegetation planted by people on beaches can prevent digging by adult females. These plants can shade the beach too much, keeping the turtle eggs from incubating, and they can block the path of hatchlings struggling toward the sea.

Death by Debris

The next time you throw away a plastic bag, toy balloon, or Styrofoam cup, think about where it may end up. Plastic trash that finds its way to the sea is often mistaken for food by green sea turtles. Plastic bags resemble jellyfish, one of the young green sea turtle's favorite meals. Once eaten, the plastic clogs the turtle's digestive system, preventing the passage of food. The turtle can starve to death as a result. As time passes, the plastics stuck in the stomach can begin to break down, releasing toxic substances that harm the turtle.

The next time you walk along a seaside boardwalk or on a beach, count how many cigarette butts you see. Though they look small and harmless, they are not. When turtles eat them, they clog their digestive systems.

▲ The back flipper of this Eastern Pacific green sea turtle was injured by a boat's propeller. The class gathered around this turtle is learning about the dangers these marine reptiles face.

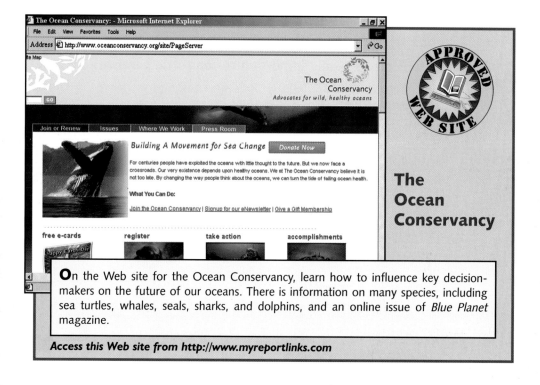

On the Web site for the Ocean Conservancy, learn how to influence key decision-makers on the future of our oceans. There is information on many species, including sea turtles, whales, seals, sharks, and dolphins, and an online issue of *Blue Planet* magazine.

Access this Web site from http://www.myreportlinks.com

▶ Light Pollution

We do not normally think of artificial lights as being a form of pollution. But the seaside lights of homes and businesses left on at night during nesting season can be deadly to adult green sea turtles and hatchlings. Brightly lit beaches can scare nesting females away from their natal beaches.

The lights can also confuse turtles, attracting adults and hatchlings inland away from the ocean. If they crawl toward streetlights, porch and deck lights, floodlights, interior lights, or car headlights, the turtles may become stranded far from water. Once they are too far inland, they are defenseless against crabs and gulls, and they are also prone to becoming dehydrated in the morning sun. Dark beaches are critically important to sea turtle survival.

Ocean Pollution

Our world's oceans are fed by thousands of rivers. Into those rivers and their tributaries flow every imaginable kind of pollution, including pesticide runoff that comes from farm fields and suburban lawns. Dioxin, mercury, and other toxic chemicals are sometimes dumped into streams by factories or leak through the ground into streams from hazardous waste sites. Untreated sewage from cities sometimes makes its way into water systems and eventually ends up in the oceans.

All kinds of pollution can kill turtles. Oil spills from refineries, tankers, and jet skis and other small craft are a major risk. Balls of tar and oil are sometimes eaten by turtles, poisoning them. These petrochemicals damage the turtle's lungs, skin, and blood. Pesticides, heavy metals, and deadly PCBs are compounds that are toxic to the environment and build up in the tissue of animals. PCBs have been found in turtle flesh and fat as well as in their eggs. They probably got there as a result of pollution absorbed by sea grasses, which are eaten by green sea turtles.

Unfortunately, the pollution problem is hard to solve because no one wants to take responsibility for causing it or pay for cleaning it up. For example, in 2001, dozens of rare green sea turtles washed up dead on Turkey's southern coast. They were most likely the victims of ocean pollution. The event created controversy because

http://www.turtles.org/h0149031.jpg - Microsoft Internet Explorer

File   Edit   View   Favorites   Tools   Help

Address   http://www.turtles.org/h0149031.jpg   Go

Fibropapillomas are tumors that sicken and often kill sea turtles. At the **Turtle Trax** Web site, learn more about the disease that causes these tumors and the people who are trying to find out its causes.

EDITOR'S CHOICE

it was difficult to tell exactly what killed the animals. The mayor of a town near the site claimed that the turtles were poisoned by toxic waste from a nearby chromium plant. He claimed that the people's local water supply was being poisoned by the same factory. But a manager at the factory denied the chromium plant's responsibility, saying all the turtles died of "naturally occurring" pollution. Environmental groups remain very concerned about the damage that ocean pollution does to sea turtles.[5]

▶ The Fibropapillomatosis Epidemic

A startling number of green sea turtles are becoming the victims of a terrible and mysterious disease called fibropapillomatosis (FP). FP is a disease in which tumors known as fibropapillomas, which can be as big as grapefruits, grow on the soft tissue of turtles. These tumors often cover the turtles' eyes, mouth, neck, or flippers. Once the turtles get this disease, they usually die from it. In the early 1970s, George Balazs, a turtle researcher who almost single-handedly saved green sea turtles in Hawaii, was the first to sound the alarm that FP was more widespread than previously thought.

Before that time, fibropapillomatosis had been a very rare disease among green sea turtles. A survey done in 1886 of twenty-five hundred green sea turtles in Florida

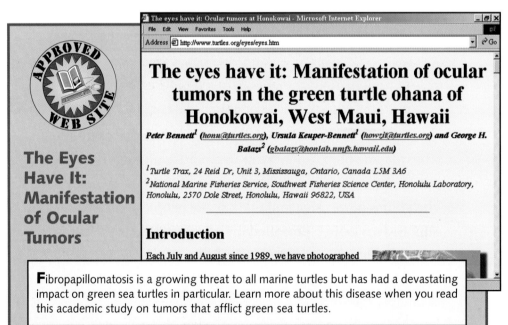

The Eyes Have It: Manifestation of Ocular Tumors

The eyes have it: Ocular tumors at Honokowai - Microsoft Internet Explorer

File   Edit   View   Favorites   Tools   Help

Address http://www.turtles.org/eyes/eyes.htm

The eyes have it: Manifestation of ocular tumors in the green turtle ohana of Honokowai, West Maui, Hawaii

Peter Bennett[1] (honu@turtles.org), Ursula Keuper-Bennett[1] (howzit@turtles.org) and George H. Balazs[2] (gbalazs@honlab.nmfs.hawaii.edu)

[1] Turtle Trax, 24 Reid Dr, Unit 3, Mississauga, Ontario, Canada L5M 3A6
[2] National Marine Fisheries Service, Southwest Fisheries Science Center, Honolulu Laboratory, Honolulu, 2570 Dole Street, Honolulu, Hawaii 96822, USA

Introduction

Each July and August since 1989, we have photographed

Fibropapillomatosis is a growing threat to all marine turtles but has had a devastating impact on green sea turtles in particular. Learn more about this disease when you read this academic study on tumors that afflict green sea turtles.

Access this Web site from http://www.myreportlinks.com

revealed no sign of the tumors. A survey of turtles in 1937 found just three turtles with FP out of two hundred examined, or just 1.5 percent. Unfortunately, tumor rates among green sea turtles have skyrocketed since then.

In one part of Florida, 40 percent of green sea turtles had FP tumors in 1980. The number infected jumped to 53 percent in 1987 and 70 percent in 1990.[6] The disease is now found in green sea turtles all over the world. If it continues to worsen, it could drive the species into extinction. And FP has also been found to infect other sea turtle species.

Some scientists think that the ocean pollution caused by humans, which has increased dramatically over the last half of the twentieth century, may be causing fibropapillomas. One hypothesis says that pollution poisons the sea grass and algae the turtles eat, causing their immune systems to fail and allowing a virus to grow uncontrollably, creating huge tumors. But this environmental toxin theory remains only a hypothesis. No one is certain what causes FP, what might cure it, or if a cure can be found in time to save the world's sea turtles.

▶ Climate Change

Another threat to green sea turtles may come from global warming, an increase in the average temperature of the earth. Our climate has changed continually over its 5-billion-year history, but most of those changes have taken place slowly over many thousands of years. In just the past one hundred years, however, the average temperature of the earth has risen 1°F (0.6°C). While that does not seem like much, climatologists, scientists who study climate, believe that the earth's average temperature will continue to increase.

Climatologists also believe that human activities are speeding up global warming because we are producing too many greenhouse gases. Greenhouse gases such as water vapor, carbon dioxide, nitrous oxide, and methane are gases that trap the sun's energy and keep it in our atmosphere, much like the panes of glass in a greenhouse trap heat. Although some of that energy escapes back into space, more and more of it is staying in our atmosphere, which results in a rise in temperature.

▶ The Threats of Global Warming

How is this warming harmful? Global warming is already beginning to melt glaciers around the world, which has started to raise ocean levels. Global warming is also heating the oceans, and since heat makes water expand, that water takes up more space, raising sea levels still further. Higher seas could completely erode or cover the beaches where green sea turtles nest. Global warming is also believed to be causing the destruction of many of the world's coral reefs, a favorite habitat and feeding ground of the green sea turtle.

Global warming may be causing another problem for the turtles. We know that the sex of a green sea turtle hatchling is determined by the temperature at which its egg is incubated inside the nest. Nest temperatures cooler than 82°F (28°C) produce all males. Temperatures higher than 88°F (31°C) produce all females. Temperatures

Sea Turtle Restoration Project: News Room - Microsoft Internet Explorer

File   Edit   View   Favorites   Tools   Help

Address http://www.seaturtles.org/   Go

HOME
DONATE
JOIN ACTIVIST NETWORK
SITEMAP

SEA TURTLE RESTORATION PROJECT

ACTIVIST'S CORNER

PROGRAMS & CAMPAIGNS

EDUCATIONAL RESOURCES

NEWSROOM

ABOUT STRP

STORE

Protecting Endangered Sea Turtles
& Marine Biodiversity Worldwide

WHAT'S NEW

Press
Releases

MTV Damaged
Sea Turtle
Beach in
Tobago

Safeway to
Offer Too Little
on Mercury
Warnings

Campaign

Sea Turtle
Restoration
Project

Done

Learn more about the plight of sea turtles and the greatest threats they face. Photographs, fact sheets on sea turtle species, information about recovery plans, and conservation reports from around the world are included on this site.

Access this Web site from http://www.myreportlinks.com

between those two extremes produce mixed clutches of females and males.

Recent studies of loggerhead turtles born on beaches from Florida to North Carolina have found that four females are being born for every one male that is born. And remember, this imbalance comes after a rise in temperature over the last century of just 1°F.

Scientists working for the United Nations estimate that human-generated emissions of greenhouse gases into the atmosphere could raise average global temperatures from 2.5 to 10.4°F (1.4 to 5.8°C) by 2100. No one knows what that might do to turtle eggs—it could cause only females to be born, or the animals could somehow adapt to the heat. Scientists do know, for example, that sea turtles have survived through times of natural global warming over the past 150 million years.

▶ Too Many Human-Caused Problems

Green sea turtles are facing the same threats that most other endangered wild animals on the earth face today. As human population grows beyond 6.4 billion people, the green sea turtle is being threatened not just by one human-caused problem, but by many.

Those threats include hunting, pollution, becoming trapped in commercial fishing lines and nets, loss of habitat, fibropapillomatosis, and global warming. Any one of these threats puts the turtles at risk, so all of them combined could push the turtles over the brink into extinction.

The large number of problems facing these animals also means that saving them is very complicated. If we work on just one problem or even two problems, without solving the rest, then the species could still die out despite our best efforts. That is why it is so important that people all over the earth begin working together to save not just a few endangered species, but entire ecosystems, and all the plants and animals that live in them.

PROTECTING GREEN SEA TURTLES

As early as 1620, people began to become concerned about the slaughter of green sea turtles. In that year, a law was passed on the island of Bermuda that in the old-fashioned-sounding language of the time was meant to end the "waste and abuse" of the turtles. It forbid people

▲ A tranquil beach in Bermuda. The people on this island realized as early as the seventeenth century that sea turtles needed some protection if they were to survive.

CCC & STSL :: Dr. Archie Carr - Microsoft Internet Explorer

File   Edit   View   Favorites   Tools   Help

Address http://www.cccturtle.org/carr.htm   Go

The history of the Caribbean Conservation Corporation (CCC) is forever intertwined with the life and accomplishments of Dr. Archie Carr. He was truly a remarkable man -- an exquisite writer, an inspiring teacher and a naturalist the likes of which may never be seen again. Dr. Carr was the founding scientific director of CCC, a role he filled until his death in 1987. Through his research, teaching and writing, Dr. Carr is responsible for accumulating and distributing much of what is known about the biology and life cycle of sea turtles. He is credited by many for bringing the first international attention to the plight of marine turtles. The brief biography presented below was written shortly after Dr. Carr's death by CCC Board member Dr. David Ehrenfeld. It was first published in the August 1987 issue of Conservation Biology, the Journal of the Society for Conservation Biology.

Archie Carr, noble spirit and greatest conservation biologist of these troubled times, died at his home on Wewa Pond near the town of Micanopy, Florida, on May 21, 1987. At the time of his death, he was the world's leading authority on sea turtles, a tropical field ecologist of exceptional skill and experience, a brilliant writer for audiences of both scientific and popular literature, a distinguished taxonomist and evolutionary biologist, and an internationally acclaimed advocate of conservation.

Archie Fairly Carr, Jr., was born on June 16, 1909, in Mobile Alabama, where his father was a Presbyterian minister and his mother a piano teacher. His keen ear for language and music developed early: as a child he learned Gullah, the lyrical dialect of coastal ...rn blacks; this linguistic ability few other whites shared. In later years he developed ...ge skills by collecting dialects from the Caribbean area and east Africa. He ...s students and many friends to anecdotes from the Mosquito coast or ...and Cayman, told in the way they had been told to him. He prided himself ..., learned from a Cuban roommate in college and perfected during his ...h Honduras and Costa Rica. After giving a series of Spanish radio ...Costa Rica on the subject of evolution, he was told by one university ...u have mastered our language."

APPROVED WEB SITE

Much of what we know about sea turtles comes from the fieldwork and writings of Dr. Archie Carr, the founding scientific director of the **Caribbean Conservation Corporation (CCC).** Learn more about the father of sea turtle research at the CCC Web site.

Done

EDITOR'S CHOICE

to "snatch & catch up indifferently all kinds of Tortoises both young and old" in order to prevent the destruction of "so excellent a fish."[1]

This "Act against the Killing of Our Young Tortoises" was the very first law passed in the New World to protect an endangered animal. Unfortunately, it had very little effect then. More than 350 years later, however, its wording did inspire Archie Carr to name his most popular and important book *The Sea Turtle—So Excellent a Fishe.* (Of course everyone, especially Archie Carr, knew that a green sea turtle is not a fish, but a reptile.)

The "Father of Sea Turtle Research"

Archie Carr was among the first scientists to recognize the plight of sea turtles. And his voice was the most eloquent in calling for them to be rescued from extinction. He did more to save sea turtles than anyone had up to that time. Many of today's sea turtle researchers either studied with Dr. Carr or with one of his students.

Archie Carr first observed sea turtles in 1947 while teaching biology in Honduras, in Central America, and it was love at first sight. In the 1950s, his pioneering sea turtle research in another Central American country, Costa Rica, led to the establishment of Tortuguero National Park, an important turtle-nesting beach. His work also led to the founding of the Caribbean Conservation Corporation, established to study and protect sea turtles.

In the 1960s, Carr launched "Operation Green Turtle" with the help of the United States Navy. The project distributed green sea turtle eggs to beaches all over the Gulf of Mexico in an effort to repopulate the Caribbean Sea with turtles. Carr tagged sea turtles so that he could learn more about their mysterious migrations.

Archie Carr also recognized that if sea turtles were to survive, their habitat would need to be protected. That is why he became outspoken in his opposition to ocean pollution.

Dr. Carr spent many years as a professor at the University of Florida. He wrote 120 scientific papers and became known as the "father of sea turtle research."

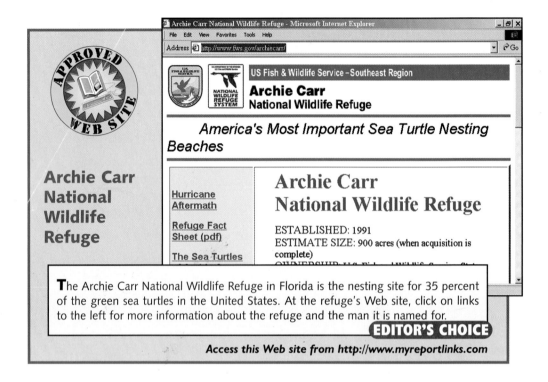

Archie Carr
National
Wildlife
Refuge

US Fish & Wildlife Service – Southeast Region

Archie Carr
National Wildlife Refuge

America's Most Important Sea Turtle Nesting Beaches

Hurricane
Aftermath

Refuge Fact
Sheet (pdf)

The Sea Turtles

Archie Carr
National Wildlife Refuge

ESTABLISHED: 1991
ESTIMATE SIZE: 900 acres (when acquisition is complete)

The Archie Carr National Wildlife Refuge in Florida is the nesting site for 35 percent of the green sea turtles in the United States. At the refuge's Web site, click on links to the left for more information about the refuge and the man it is named for.

EDITOR'S CHOICE

Access this Web site from http://www.myreportlinks.com

Though he died in 1987, his legacy lives on in Florida's Archie Carr National Wildlife Refuge, a 20-mile beach and sea turtle nesting site. Carr's legacy also inspired the public to take up the challenge of saving the world's sea turtles.

Public Awareness and Action

Starting in the 1970s, people became especially concerned when the green sea turtle population plummeted. Environmentalists watched as the number of breeding females plunged. They were able to convince governments to pass laws to protect these creatures.

Today, a web of international treaties and national laws are meant to safeguard green sea turtles. These laws, though imperfect and sometimes poorly enforced,

A United States Fish and Wildlife Service employee on Pelican Island, Florida, with a young green sea turtle. This government agency plays an important role in sea turtle conservation and management.

offer sea turtles some hope of survival. The United States and Costa Rica have passed some of the toughest laws protecting these ocean-going reptiles.

Unfortunately, many other countries still have no laws protecting turtles. As a result, a green sea turtle that is born on a protected beach in Costa Rica may end up swimming into waters where it is not protected from turtle hunters.

The Endangered Species Act Protects Green Sea Turtles

The Endangered Species Act (ESA) was passed by the United States Congress and signed into law by President Richard Nixon in 1973 as a way of protecting animals and plants that were in danger of becoming extinct. The green sea turtle was listed as endangered within United States territories and waters on July 28, 1978. The ESA prohibits the hunting, capture, possession, sale, injuring, or harassment of green sea turtles and imposes stiff fines and criminal penalties against people who violate the law. Under the act, money and land can be used to aid in green sea turtle conservation efforts.

The United States Fish and Wildlife Service (FWS) enforces the ESA, protecting endangered animals and plants on land. The National Marine Fisheries Service (NMFS), part of the National Oceanic and Atmospheric Administration (NOAA), enforces the ESA for ocean plants and animals. Since green sea turtles are found on both land and sea, they are supposed to be protected by both agencies.

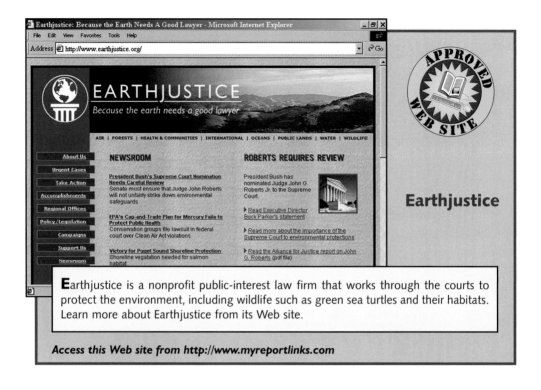

Earthjustice is a nonprofit public-interest law firm that works through the courts to protect the environment, including wildlife such as green sea turtles and their habitats. Learn more about Earthjustice from its Web site.

Access this Web site from http://www.myreportlinks.com

But some environmental groups do not think that the federal government is doing a good job protecting green sea turtles. In 2001, for example, environmental groups including the Turtle Island Restoration Network and the Center for Marine Conservation sued the NMFS for failing to protect green sea turtles from longline fishing in Hawaii.

Some environmental groups say that the agencies are too interested in protecting commercial fishing and not interested enough in following the law to protect endangered species like the green sea turtle. "We are watching these animals disappear from the Earth forever before our eyes. We cannot allow the government agency responsible for their recovery to turn its back and ignore the law," said Earthjustice attorney Paul Achitoff. Earthjustice is a nonprofit public-interest law firm whose lawyers handle environmental cases.[2]

Threats to the Endangered Species Act

Unfortunately, some members of Congress and some large developers and corporations are pushing for the repeal of the Endangered Species Act. They say that it inhibits economic growth and ties up new construction projects. If the developers and big corporations win and Congress repeals or weakens the law, the green sea turtle and many other endangered species could be put on a fast road to extinction.

Many people think that the repeal of the law would not only be bad for the animals themselves but also for people. Green sea turtles, for example, draw many tourists to places like Florida and Hawaii. In fact, green sea turtles are so important to the tourist economy of Hawaii that they are given protection by state laws that are even tougher than the federal Endangered Species Act.

In Hawaii it is illegal for swimmers or divers to ride sea turtles or bother them in any way. Fines for violating this state law can be as high as one hundred thousand dollars and can even include prison time. Hawaii's turtle laws were created with the hope that green sea turtles and other kinds of sea turtles will not only be saved from extinction but will also be restored to their previous numbers, benefiting the turtles and Hawaii's tourism industry.

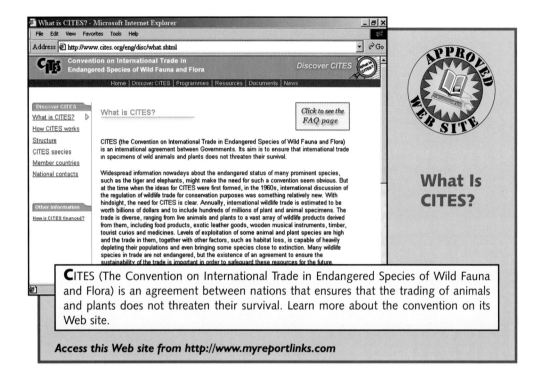

APPROVED WEB SITE

What Is CITES?

CITES (The Convention on International Trade in Endangered Species of Wild Fauna and Flora) is an agreement between nations that ensures that the trading of animals and plants does not threaten their survival. Learn more about the convention on its Web site.

Access this Web site from http://www.myreportlinks.com

▷ International Treaties Protect Turtles

During the 1960s, people began to realize that one of the greatest threats to the world's wildlife was the trade in endangered species between countries. A big threat to green sea turtles at that time was trade in tortoiseshell jewelry.

To block this trade and reduce the risk of species going extinct, an international agreement between governments known as the Convention on International Trade in Endangered Species of Wild Fauna and Flora (CITES) was adopted. In 1963, CITES was drafted as a resolution of the IUCN, the International Union for the Conservation of Nature and Natural Resources, now known as the World Conservation Union.

It took ten years before the text of the convention was agreed upon by eighty member countries, known as parties, and two more years, until 1975, before it began to be enforced. Every nation that signed the treaty agreed to make laws within their own countries to protect the endangered animals and plants. Today, 167 parties participate by regulating the international trade of wildlife to ensure its survival.

CITES protects green sea turtles by classifying them as an "Appendix I" animal, which means the species is threatened with extinction and cannot be traded between countries. There are now seven hundred species listed in

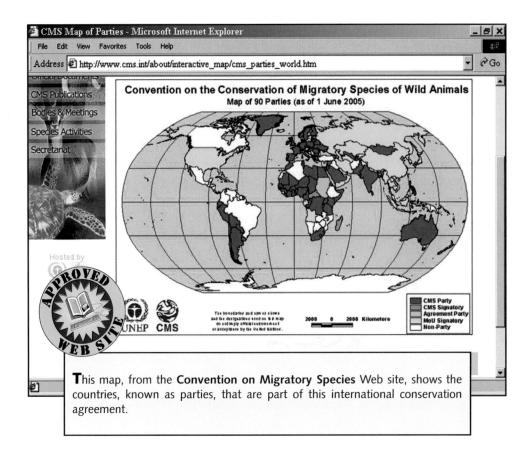

This map, from the **Convention on Migratory Species** Web site, shows the countries, known as parties, that are part of this international conservation agreement.

Appendix I, which includes the great whales, great apes, rhinoceroses, elephants, big cats, and all sea turtles.

The Inter-American Convention for the Protection and Conservation of Sea Turtles is a new international treaty whose goal is "to promote the protection, conservation and recovery of sea turtle populations and of the habitats on which they depend."[3] It is the only international treaty devoted exclusively to the protection of all seven species of sea turtles and their habitats. The treaty has already been signed by twelve nations, including the United States, and nine of those have fully ratified it, making it law. If the terms of the treaty are adhered to by all the nations that have signed it, it should do a lot to protect green sea turtles and their nesting beaches.

Another international treaty protects green sea turtles. The Convention on the Conservation of Migratory Species of Wild Animals, known also by its shortened name, the Convention on Migratory Species (CMS), is an agreement of ninety member nations administered by the United Nations Environment Programme to protect migrating species throughout their entire range. Green sea turtles are protected under this treaty because they make long migrations from their feeding grounds to their nesting grounds. The fate of green sea turtles is not secure, however, since some countries are doing a lot to protect the species while other countries are doing much less.

Another Advocate for Sea Turtles

When Karen Bjorndal was a child, her aunt bought her a red-eared slider turtle. From caring for that pet grew a

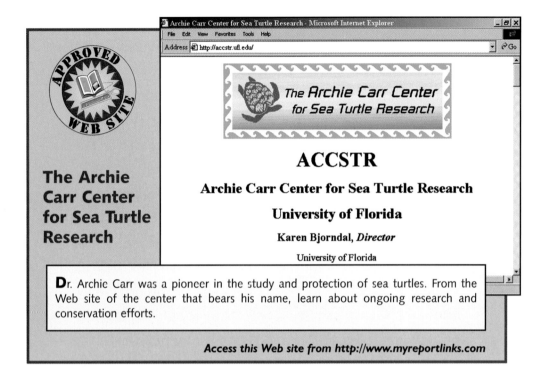

Access this Web site from http://www.myreportlinks.com

The Archie Carr Center for Sea Turtle Research

ACCSTR

Archie Carr Center for Sea Turtle Research

University of Florida

Karen Bjorndal, *Director*

University of Florida

Dr. Archie Carr was a pioneer in the study and protection of sea turtles. From the Web site of the center that bears his name, learn about ongoing research and conservation efforts.

passion for sea turtles. At the University of Florida, Bjorndal studied with the legendary Archie Carr, and she went on to become one of his most gifted students. As a graduate student, she studied the diets of green sea turtles and in the process became like a mother to them: She actually "diapered" the turtles so that she could collect their feces to analyze the foods they ate. She is now the director of the Archie Carr Center for Sea Turtle Research at the University of Florida.

One of Bjorndal's most important discoveries was that the extinction of green sea turtles could change the ecology of tropical oceans all over the planet. Green sea turtles play a key role in improving sea-grass habitats. By grazing on sea grass, the turtles act like gardeners. Their "cropping" of the sea grass—eating part of the plant, but not killing it—causes the plant to grow new shoots, which are more tender and higher in nutrition than the older tougher parts of the plant. Sea-grass cropping by turtles produces sea-grass patches that then become preferred feeding areas for all kinds of fish and other sea life.

This and other research gives conservationists new reasons to argue for the preservation of green sea turtles. It shows that green sea turtles are not only beautiful creatures but are also vital in keeping ecosystems healthy, productive, and balanced. Healthy ocean ecosystems are not only good for the creatures living in them. They also mean bigger catches for commercial fishing fleets and a steady, sustainable supply of fish for people to eat.

▶ You Can Adopt a Turtle!

Turtle researchers like Karen Bjorndal are not working alone to save green sea turtles. There are also many non-profit environmental groups working to protect these animals, and most of them are just a mouse-click away.

The Caribbean Conservation Corporation and Sea Turtle Survival League (CCC) is one of the best-known sea turtle organizations in the world. Founded by Archie Carr, it works to enact laws to protect sea turtles and provide sanctuaries for them. It also leads turtle research in Costa Rica and Florida.

Among the group's many programs is one that a school class could become involved in: The Adopt-a-Turtle program. Your class could hold a fund-raising event with

The Watamu Turtle Watch of Kenya is a conservation organization committed to protecting the sea turtles that nest on this African nation's beaches. At the group's site, learn more about their efforts, which include an "Adopt-a-Turtle" program.

Access this Web site from http://www.myreportlinks.com

the proceeds going as a donation to the CCC. For this donation, your class gets a membership card and sea turtle conservation guide and you are entitled to adopt and name a turtle. CCC researchers tag the turtle with the name you select for it at their research station in Costa Rica. With a "Name Your Own Turtle Adoption," you are the only person to adopt that turtle. You are also notified when, or if, researchers spot your turtle again.

Even more exciting, CCC members can follow a sea turtle on its migrations on the web. Some named turtles have small satellite transmitters attached to the backs of their shells. By logging on to the CCC Web site, you can track turtles as they move from foraging grounds to nesting sites.

The Watamu Turtle Watch (WTW), in Kenya, Africa, also allows you to adopt green sea turtles through a small donation. This conservation group offers adoptions for turtles just released from local fishing nets. You can even adopt an entire sea turtle nest.[4] The WTW was formed in 1997 to continue the efforts begun in the 1970s by a local naturalist to conserve marine turtles in the Watamu Marine Park and along the northern shores of a creek. It also offered a program to educate local people about the need to save Kenya's marine turtles. But it soon became apparent that the turtles' entire range and Kenya's waters needed to be preserved from things like overfishing, development, and pollution. So in 2002, the

WTW Programmes - Microsoft Internet Explorer

File   Edit   View   Favorites   Tools   Help

Address http://www.watamuturtles.com/WTW_Programmes.htm   Go

Turtle rehabilitation

In 2003 WTW set up a simple rehabilitation facility where sick turtles can be cared for and rehabilitated back into the wild. Each year WTW is brought sick and injured turtles, which previously we were unable to treat. WTW has linked up with a local vet to provide the necessary medical advice.

a juvenile green turtle out of the rehab tank and in feeding position with Kahindi

Sick sea turtles in Kenya's waters are cared for in facilities set up by the **Watamu Turtle Watch.** Learn more about this group at its Web site.

Local Ocean Trust, a charitable organization, was born. It works closely with Kenyan government agencies and other conservation groups and now oversees the work of the WTW.

Other Ways to Help

You can also join the effort to protect sea turtles by going to Turtle Trax, a Web site that is a gateway to sites on turtle research and turtle conservation organizations around the world.[5] Turtle Trax also links to the Amazing Hawaiian SeaTurtleCam, which offers an opportunity for school groups and families to organize a turtle-viewing party from anywhere in the world.[6] This webcam allows you to watch green sea turtles swimming and foraging in their Hawaiian habitat. You can also use the videos to launch a discussion about turtle preservation.

Learn more about turtles and spark discussion on how to save them by going to Seaturtle.org and checking out their newsletters as well as hundreds of digital images of sea turtles.[7] These amazing pictures document the complete life cycle of sea turtles. Once you have learned as much as you can about this species, then you can take action.

Becoming a Sea Turtle Activist

You might begin by organizing an e-mail letter-writing campaign to let your senators and representatives know that you think they should not allow the Endangered Species Act to be weakened or repealed. You can find the addresses of your federal and state government officials

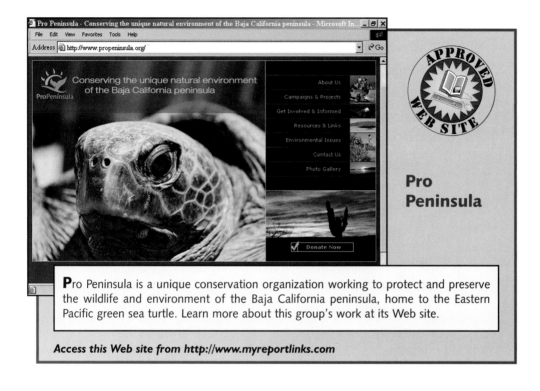

Pro Peninsula is a unique conservation organization working to protect and preserve the wildlife and environment of the Baja California peninsula, home to the Eastern Pacific green sea turtle. Learn more about this group's work at its Web site.

Access this Web site from http://www.myreportlinks.com

at Congress.org, or you may be able to find them in a phone book or in your local newspaper.[8]

You could also mention that TED laws should be better enforced so that all shrimpers and flounder trawlers stop catching and killing turtles. And you could contact officials in communities where there are turtle nesting beaches and find out what they are doing to protect turtle nests. Do they, for example, ask people to turn off their outdoor lights during nesting season?

Another way to save green sea turtles is by volunteering to help researchers tag turtles, count eggs, take measurements, or help at government turtle hatcheries. While these programs require that participants be adults, that does not mean that you and your class cannot raise money to sponsor a teacher, parent, or other adult to volunteer with the Caribbean Conservation Corporation or another group.

The sea turtle biologists of the CCC are supported by adult volunteers on the beach at Tortuguero, Costa Rica. Volunteers there are helping scientists unlock the remaining mysteries about Tortuguero's green sea turtles. Another group that sponsors similar programs is the Earthwatch Institute, which calls for the help of adult volunteers in protecting green sea turtles in Malaysia and other places.[9]

If you raise money to fund a volunteer for the CCC or Earthwatch, that volunteer can report back on his or her adventures with green sea turtles by sending an e-mail

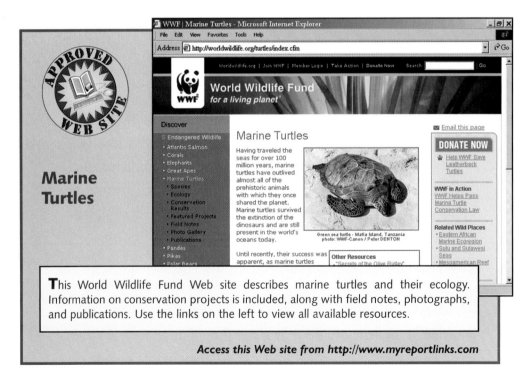

Marine
Turtles

This World Wildlife Fund Web site describes marine turtles and their ecology. Information on conservation projects is included, along with field notes, photographs, and publications. Use the links on the left to view all available resources.

Access this Web site from http://www.myreportlinks.com

▲ Pro Peninsula introduces kids in the San Diego Bay area to an Eastern Pacific green sea turtle. Programs like this help people care about the wildlife around them so that they will understand the need to preserve it.

and digital photos. This person could also prepare a speech or presentation when he or she returns home. This team approach to saving green sea turtles has the chance to be very successful.

Changing the Way We Do Business

You could also organize a campaign to raise awareness about how many turtles die when they eat trash like plastic bags or Styrofoam cups. You could begin with a letter-writing campaign to corporations that encourages them to develop plastic products that are biodegradable, able to break down into materials that do not harm the environment once they are thrown away.

We could all profit if businesses worked to find new products and methods that did not harm green sea turtles. It would be great if fishing tackle companies developed a brand of fishing line monofilament that was biodegradable after being exposed to water for several weeks. Entanglement in plastic monofilament fishing line may have killed as many as seven hundred sea turtles in Florida in 1999. Often it is not that difficult to develop such new products. There only needs to be a demand for them. You could help to create that demand.

Another project might be to write to companies that manufacture plastics to encourage them to become more involved in recycling their many products. You could make the endangered green sea turtle the focus of your letter-writing campaign. Another idea would be to organize a plastics recycling campaign in your school, neighborhood, or town that emphasizes the plight of the sea turtle.

▲ *An artificial reef in Pokai Bay, Oahu, Hawaii, provides habitat for this young green sea turtle. Artificial reefs often are made up of sunken vessels, and they provide marine life with homes, protection, and feeding grounds.*

▲ *Gliding through the ocean depths, this sea turtle, its flippers extended, looks as though it is flying.*

How about a working vacation? The next time your family travels to the seashore, why not spend some time removing debris from the beach. Put on a pair of gloves and gather up plastic cups, bottles, bags, and fishing line and dispose of them properly. Even if the beach you are staying at is not a turtle nesting beach or if your vacation takes you to a river but not the sea, your cleanup still matters. It prevents that plastic from being washed into the water, eventually carried out into the ocean, and eaten by a sea turtle or other marine animal.

There is no reason that our trash should end up in the ocean and kill green sea turtles. If we all get informed and work together, we could begin to eliminate the garbage in our oceans.

Celebrate the Green Sea Turtle

Green sea turtles are impressive creatures. The more you spread the word and celebrate this endangered species, the more people will be won over to help preserve it. Green sea turtles are ancient reptiles that go back to the days of the dinosaurs. They are great migrators and divers, and they can stay under water for more than an hour. But they cannot survive without our help. Humans have put green sea turtles at risk. Humans working together can save them.

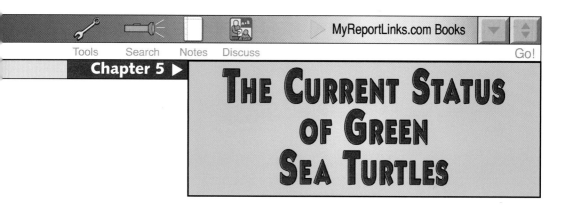

Chapter 5

THE CURRENT STATUS OF GREEN SEA TURTLES

When one considers how many millions of green sea turtles there once were and the many human-made and natural threats these animals face every day, it is not surprising that green sea turtles are considered an endangered species.

The IUCN-World Conservation Union publishes a list known as the Red List of all the animals and plants threatened with extinction on the earth. Green sea turtles have been on the Red List for more than four decades. The IUCN says that the number of green sea turtles continues to decline in all of the world's oceans. They point to findings that show a decline between 48 percent and 67 percent worldwide, over three generations, in the number of mature females that have nested.[1]

Hunting remains the most serious problem. Egg collection still happens at 45 percent of all nesting beaches. On some Indonesian islands, 100 percent of all turtle eggs are harvested. In the Philippines, up to half are taken. The loss of these thousands of eggs means that twenty-five years from now, there will be few mature turtles around to mate and produce young.

At the same time, juvenile and adult green sea turtles are still being harvested for food. Between five thousand

Pro Peninsula researchers measure the carapace of an Eastern Pacific green sea turtle. Despite the group's efforts, green sea turtles in the waters off Baja California are still being killed for food.

and ten thousand green sea turtles are killed each year in their foraging grounds around Baja California. But these numbers are small when compared with the one hundred thousand turtles killed every year in Southeast Asia. Considering all this evidence of impending extinction, says James Spotila, "It seems incredible that people still eat thousands of green turtles every year."[2]

▶ Hope for the World's Green Sea Turtles

The IUCN-World Conservation Union offers some hope for green sea turtles. A growing awareness of the dangers that green sea turtles face has caused many scientists, environmentalists, and government officials to work together to save them.

As a result, many of the human impacts on turtles have begun to decrease. Egg and turtle hunting has decreased in many nesting and foraging locations around the world. The use of TEDs has helped a lot in the United States as well as in Central America and South America, though many nations still do not require them. Community programs are also helping slow the take of turtles and their eggs.

For those reasons, green sea turtle populations in the Caribbean and the North Atlantic Ocean seem to be seeing a slight upturn. The number of green sea turtles in the Gulf of Mexico has increased. Other parts of the world, however, are not seeing as much improvement.

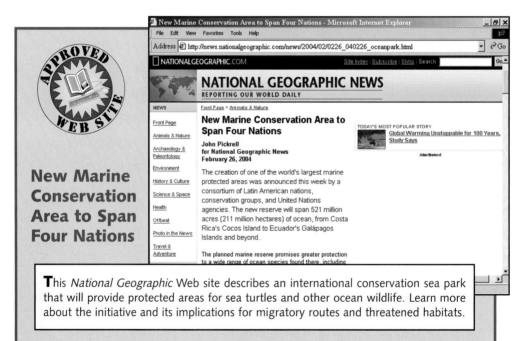

This *National Geographic* Web site describes an international conservation sea park that will provide protected areas for sea turtles and other ocean wildlife. Learn more about the initiative and its implications for migratory routes and threatened habitats.

Access this Web site from http://www.myreportlinks.com

Communities Take Action

Ecotourism has become an important source of income for some sea turtle communities. As a result, local people have become more interested in protecting turtles and their eggs than harvesting them. One slaughterhouse in Mexico, where fifty thousand turtles a year were once killed so they could be made into purses and shoes, was recently turned into a sea turtle museum to educate people about endangered sea turtles. At Punta Banco, Costa Rica, ecotourist dollars help operate a community-run turtle hatchery program.[3]

Progress in the Americas

Sea turtle conservationist Peter Pritchard, named a "Hero of the Planet" in 2000 by *Time* magazine, has worked with Arawak Indian communities in Guyana, in South America, to save green sea turtles. He devised a government program that turned green sea turtle hunters into chicken farmers: He got the Arawak to stop eating turtles and start eating chicken. Pritchard also hires Arawak people to tag turtles at his research station, creating strong community allies for the animals. Pritchard told *Time* that the killing stopped not because new laws were imposed but because families had come to value living turtles over dead ones.[4]

Brazil's Project Tamar, run by Maria Angela Marcovaldi, sets an example for other community sea turtle projects.[5] This program, supported by the Brazilian government and nonprofit groups, has been protecting sea turtles for nearly twenty-five years. The project's name comes from **Ta**rtaruga **Ma**rinha, Portuguese for "sea turtle." It hires the same fishermen who once hunted and harvested turtles to protect them. Today, twelve hundred fishermen and their relatives in local seaside villages have been recruited to staff twenty stations that monitor 621 miles (1,000 kilometers) of sea turtle nesting beaches in eight Brazilian states. Project Tamar has created an industry based on saving sea turtles. Its staff provides environmental education, gives technical assistance to fishermen, gets villagers to plant vegetable gardens as an alternative source of food, and sets up factories where villagers make T-shirts, caps, backpacks, and other souvenirs that sport sea turtle logos. The organization has even created a national Turtle Day plus other sea turtle celebrations. It is responsible for making Brazil's sea turtle habitat a popular ecotourism destination.

Other Partnerships

In Costa Rica, partnerships between local people, scientists, and the government are paying off. At Tortuguero National Park, the turtle nests have slowly begun to increase. The number of green sea turtles in this rookery dwindled in the 1960s as local people harvested and sold turtles for the turtle soup market. Archie Carr and the researchers of the Caribbean Conservation Corporation convinced the government to make Tortuguero a protected national park in the 1970s. The CCC and the government have hired local people as beach monitors to count turtle tracks and have trained them as sea turtle nesting beach guides. The local philosophy has changed, with

Sea Turtles - Microsoft Internet Explorer

File   Edit   View   Favorites   Tools   Help

Address http://www.seaworld.org/infobooks/SeaTurtle/home.html   Go

Sea Turtles

Contents

Scientific Classification
Habitat and Distribution
Physical Characteristics
Senses
Adaptations for an Aquatic Environment
Behavior
Diet and Eating Habits
Reproduction
Hatching and Hatchlings
Longevity and Causes of Death
Conservation
Bibliography

Sea Turtles

This SeaWorld site offers an online book on sea turtles, which gives information on turtles' senses, causes of death, and diet. An index and a bibliography for further reading are included.

Access this Web site from http://www.myreportlinks.com

Tortuguero residents seeing turtles as worth more alive than in the stewpot. This change has resulted in a great success: Over the last forty years, Tortuguero has become an important green sea turtle rookery and turtle eco-tourism destination.[6]

In Florida, residents up and down the coast have organized to pass ordinances that control lighting near beaches during the nesting season. Floridians have also organized to clean their beaches and to monitor and protect sea turtle nests. The Amelia Island Sea Turtle Watch is a good example of how Florida is protecting its turtles.[7] Its volunteers are trained each year to survey the island's beaches and collect data about nesting activity. When necessary, the group relocates turtle clutches from areas

▲ *A honu swims in the waters off the Hawaiian Islands. Green sea turtles feature prominently in the islands' mythology.*

where they are in danger of being destroyed by beach traffic or development to safer beaches. Volunteers also report stranded turtles in order to get medical attention for them and get them back in the water. And they have even worked with the U.S. Army Corps of Engineers to minimize harm from beach sand replenishment. Hawaii has similar programs, such as the World Turtle Trust's Honu Project. (*Honu* is Hawaiian for "sea turtle.")[8]

Commercial Fishing and Turtles

The struggle between commercial fishermen and green sea turtle defenders continues. The result of that struggle could determine whether green sea turtles survive or not—and whether the fishermen stay in business.

In 2005, the countries of Costa Rica, Croatia, and Sweden joined more than 800 scientists from 83 countries and 230 environmental organizations in calling for a ban on longline fishing. They also proposed the creation of a network of high seas Marine Protected Areas in the Pacific Ocean.[9]

Fishermen fear that this will destroy their livelihood. But environmentalists argue that the banning of longline fishing and the establishment of the preserves will not only help green sea turtles. It will also increase the numbers of fish in unprotected areas, and that should help commercial fishermen, too.

"Industrial longline fishing is a loss-loss situation not only for sea turtles but also [for] those who rely on the ocean for their food and livelihood," writes scientist and environmentalist Robert Ovetz. A recent report found that industrial longline fishing in the Pacific catches and kills an estimated 4.4 million sea turtles, sharks, marine mammals, billfish (fish with slender jaws, such as marlins and sailfish), and seabirds each year. At that rate, all of those animals could quickly disappear. "Closing areas of the ocean off from industrial fishing is good for fisheries and turtles," Ovetz says.[10]

http://www.cccturtle.org/media/tort-sat-gr.jpg - Microsoft Internet Explorer

File   Edit   View   Favorites   Tools   Help

Address   http://www.cccturtle.org/media/tort-sat-gr.jpg

The transmitter attached to the carapace of this green sea turtle does not harm the animal. This photo and others are found on the Web site of the **Caribbean Conservation Corporation.**

Other ideas to curb accidental and illegal sea turtle catches are to put government observers aboard fishing boats and to use satellites to track suspicious ships that might be netting turtles illegally.

Ongoing Turtle Research

The more we know about an animal, the more likely we are not to harm it and instead find ways to help it. That is why research into the still-mysterious life cycle of green sea turtles is so important. Until recently, most research on green sea turtles was conducted on turtles at nesting beaches. But since turtles spend more than 90 percent of their time in the water, most of their activities have gone unseen.

Scientists are using innovative techniques to learn about sea turtle life in the ocean. For example, the long migrations made by green sea turtles between their feeding grounds and breeding grounds have remained mostly a mystery until very recently. The use of satellite telemetry has begun to change that. Researchers recently began attaching small platform terminal transmitters (PTT) to green sea turtle shells. PTTs look like small radios with short antennas. As the turtle swims deep beneath the surface of the ocean, the PTT collects all kinds of data: the direction the turtle is swimming, the route it is taking, the temperature of the water it is in, how often it surfaces, and more. Each time the turtle

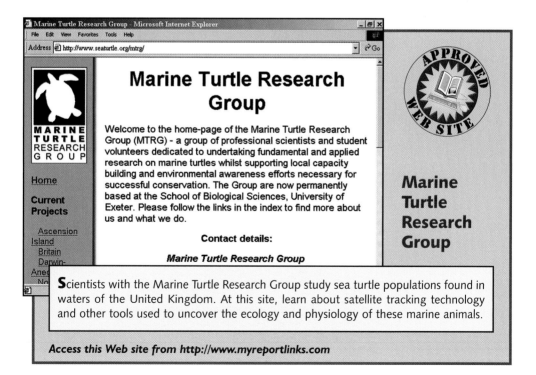

Marine Turtle Research Group - Microsoft Internet Explorer

File   Edit   View   Favorites   Tools   Help

Address   http://www.seaturtle.org/mtrg/   Go

Marine Turtle Research Group

MARINE TURTLE RESEARCH GROUP

Home

Current Projects

Ascension Island
Britain
Darwin-
Ane
No

Welcome to the home-page of the Marine Turtle Research Group (MTRG) - a group of professional scientists and student volunteers dedicated to undertaking fundamental and applied research on marine turtles whilst supporting local capacity building and environmental awareness efforts necessary for successful conservation. The Group are now permanently based at the School of Biological Sciences, University of Exeter. Please follow the links in the index to find more about us and what we do.

Contact details:

Marine Turtle Research Group

Marine Turtle Research Group

Scientists with the Marine Turtle Research Group study sea turtle populations found in waters of the United Kingdom. At this site, learn about satellite tracking technology and other tools used to uncover the ecology and physiology of these marine animals.

Access this Web site from http://www.myreportlinks.com

An Eastern Pacific green sea turtle is carried ashore in Baja California Sur, Mexico, to be measured, weighed, and tagged by members of Grupo Tortuguero, a sea turtle conservation network. This group monitors the status of sea turtle populations in the waters surrounding the peninsula.

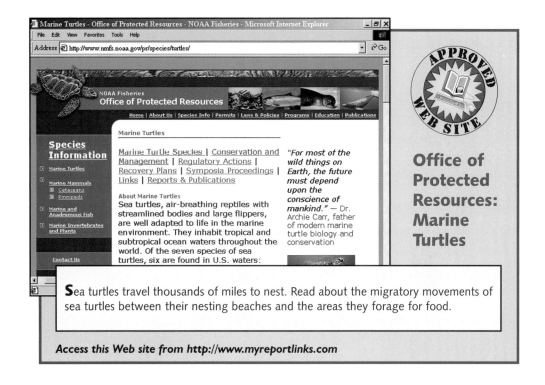

Sea turtles travel thousands of miles to nest. Read about the migratory movements of sea turtles between their nesting beaches and the areas they forage for food.

Access this Web site from http://www.myreportlinks.com

surfaces for air, the PTT sends its stored data to an orbiting satellite. The satellite sends the turtle data to a ground station, which sends it to a computer for scientists to study. Thanks to satellite telemetry, scientists are beginning to map the migration patterns of the world's green sea turtles. This knowledge could be very helpful in saving turtles by helping people develop plans to clean up pollution hot spots where turtles frequently travel.

Important research is also under way to find the cause and cure for fibropapillomatosis, new ways to keep sea turtles out of fishing nets, and better techniques for hatching and raising turtles in captivity at sea turtle hatcheries.

Chapter 6 ▶

CAN WE SAVE GREEN SEA TURTLES AND THE SEAS?

It is becoming clear to scientists and environmentalists that saving the green sea turtle is going to be a huge job. That is because if we are to save green sea turtles, we must also save all of the places in which they live, and they live in lots of places. They float through vast open oceans when young, feed in the shallows along seacoasts and in coral reefs as juveniles, and then migrate long distances to return to the beach where they were born and where they will nest. In order to save the green sea turtle, we must save all of these diverse habitats. We must literally save all of the world's oceans.

▶ Poisoning Our Oceans

Unfortunately, our oceans are in big trouble. Humans have had a negative impact on our oceans, causing coral reefs to die, sea-grass beds to shrink, beaches to be developed, and populations of fish, sea mammals, and reptiles to diminish. As the world's human population grows, more and more communities worldwide dump their sewage, chemical poisons, and other pollutants into the rivers that flow into the seas.

Even cities such as New York City, where technological advancements are commonplace, have not solved

▲ This coral reef in the Florida Keys is home to an endangered sea turtle—and a human observer, watching the turtle's movements.

All species of sea turtles found in the world are either threatened or endangered. For information on the biology, conservation, and recovery plans for these ocean reptiles, visit this Australian government site.

Access this Web site from http://www.myreportlinks.com

their pollution problems. New York, like many American cities, has combined sewer overflows (CSOs) that carry both rainwater and sewage to waste-treatment plants. This system works very well in dry weather, but during big storms, the rush of storm water overwhelms the treatment plant's ability to clean up the pollution. When that happens, thousands of tons of raw sewage flood into the rivers and bays and eventually into the ocean.

Some scientists think that the poisons we put into the oceans are already seriously affecting sea creatures, weakening their immune systems and making them vulnerable to diseases that they could normally resist.

Some research is showing a relationship between badly polluted coastal waters and the fibropapilloma tumors that kill green sea turtles. Jakarta Bay in Indonesia is one of the most polluted bodies of water on earth, and turtles living there have a much higher rate of FP than turtles living in nearby clean waters. Some researchers think that pollution is helping normally rare viruses to become more numerous. The viruses release a poison that is absorbed into the sea grasses. The turtles eat the toxic sea grass and later develop the FP tumors.

Scientists also think that the more that people degrade the oceans, the worse such marine diseases will become and the more likely it will be for more species to go extinct. Since the 1980s, as ocean conditions have worsened, the seas have been swept by new and terrible diseases. Mysterious, widespread, and devastating epidemics have killed dolphins, whales, porpoises, seals, sea

The Sea Turtle Research Program of the Southwest Marine Fisheries Service studies sea turtle migrations and habitat use, among other things. Read more about their findings on this NOAA site.

Access this Web site from http://www.myreportlinks.com

turtles, sea urchins, and other marine species. More than twenty-five such epidemics were recorded by researchers between 1980 and 1997. Only seven serious epidemics occurred between 1931 and 1980, when people and pollution were having much less impact on the oceans.

The Consequences of Species Decline

The loss of key species, like the green sea turtle, can have far-reaching impacts on the health of the oceans. For example, green sea turtles and sea urchins used to control the growth of algae in the Caribbean Sea. But with sea turtles in decline, and after a major disease epidemic wiped out the sea urchins in the 1980s, algae began to grow out of control and smothered many Caribbean coral reefs. That harmed the fish and other creatures that live on the reefs.

"What we're witnessing could be described as an epidemic of epidemics—call it a 'metademic'—in the ocean realm," writes Osha Gray Davidson. "Marine epidemics are burning through a host of life forms from plants to invertebrates to marine mammals, threatening ocean biodiversity on a scale unprecedented in modern times."[1]

The Need to Act Now

Davidson and many marine biologists believe that all of the world's oceans may be endangered. The seas, where all life originated and which still feed millions of people, may be dying. "If we don't act quickly," writes Davidson, "Our children may inherit an imposter ocean, a sickly ghost, drained of animal life and crowded with pathogens

Researchers from the Southwest Marine Fisheries Service carry a large green sea turtle onto shore from San Diego Bay. The survival of this species is, truly, in our hands.

SEATURTLE.ORG - Microsoft Internet Explorer

File Edit View Favorites Tools Help

Address http://www.seaturtle.org/

seaturtle.org

ImageLib Maptool Tracking Mail Members News Links Search Help Donate

MTN   Symposium   Directory   Bookstore   Resources   Partners

Site Search

advanced search...

Sign In

Currently Online
Users: 1
Guest 18

Recent Favorites

Satellite Tracking
The World According To Me...
Marine Turtle Newsletter
Image Library
Manjula G
Blogging

SEATURTLE.ORG eNews

Adopt a Sea Turtle

Support Marine Conservation
Give a gift that counts.

Get the latest news and updates!

Headlines
subscribe   Sea turtle no longer sending signals

Support seaturtle.org

SEATURTLE.ORG made possible in part with support from:

● Florida Cooperative Fish & Wildlife Research Unit
● nancy stegens
● Maria Leonor Sardinha
● Karen Frutchey

Help support seaturtle.org programs.

Seaturtle.org

This is a good site for information concerning the conservation, science, biology, habitat, legal status, management, and future of all sea turtle species. Click on the image library for photos you can use in your report.

Access this Web site from http://www.myreportlinks.com

[diseases]. The turtle plague of fibropapillomatosis is a flashing red light alerting us to marine problems."[2]

James Spotila agrees. "The future for green turtles is uncertain," he writes. "If nothing changes they will likely become extinct in most of the world during this century, holding on in a few places where protection is strong. If we act, however, they may soon reach the bottom of their decline and begin to climb. If so it will result from practical steps taken one beach, one country, one law, one village at a time. And it will have been worth it."[3]

In 1973, Congress took the farsighted step of creating the Endangered Species Act, widely regarded as the world's strongest and most effective wildlife conservation law. It set an ambitious goal: to reverse the alarming trend of human-caused extinction that threatened the ecosystems we all share.

Each book in this series explores the life of an endangered animal. The books tell how and why the animals have become endangered and explain the efforts being made to restore their populations.

The United States Fish and Wildlife Service and the National Marine Fisheries Service share responsibility for administration of the Endangered Species Act. Over time, animals are added to, reclassified in, or removed from the federal list of Endangered and Threatened Wildlife and Plants. At the time of publication, all the animals in this series were listed as endangered species. The most up-to-date list can be found at **http://www.fws.gov/endangered/wildlife.html**.

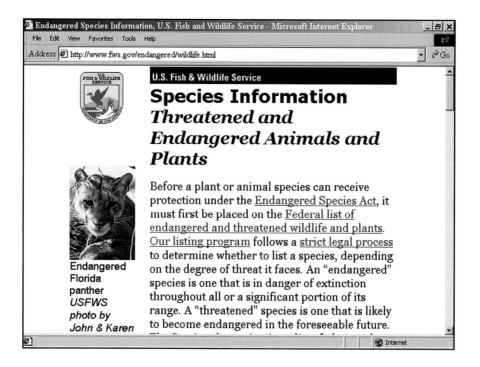

Report Links

The Internet sites described below can be accessed at http://www.myreportlinks.com

▶**Turtle Trax**
Editor's Choice This site is dedicated to providing information about sea turtles.

▶**Caribbean Conservation Corporation and Sea Turtle Survival League**
Editor's Choice This group works to protect sea turtles and their habitats.

▶**Green Sea Turtle—*Chelonia mydas***
Editor's Choice Learn how green sea turtles differ from other sea turtles.

▶**A Night With a Nesting Green Turtle**
Editor's Choice This site takes a look at a nesting green sea turtle.

▶**Archie Carr National Wildlife Refuge**
Editor's Choice Learn about an important protected nesting site for green sea turtles.

▶**Office of Naval Research—Ocean Life: Green Sea Turtle**
Editor's Choice U.S. naval scientists offer a glimpse under the ocean.

▶**Adopt a Sea Turtle**
Adopting a sea turtle can ensure its protection and survival.

▶**The Archie Carr Center for Sea Turtle Research**
Find out more about sea turtles and the efforts to save them at this University of Florida center.

▶**Convention on Migratory Species**
This international treaty protects migratory species.

▶**Earthjustice**
Learn about a law firm that works to protect the environment.

▶**The Eyes Have It: Manifestation of Ocular Tumors in the Green Turtle**
Read about the plight of diseased Hawaiian green sea turtles.

▶**Marine Species Conservation: Marine Turtles**
Learn about sea turtles and marine conservation from this site.

▶**Marine Turtle Research Group**
The MTRG studies marine turtle ecology and its secrets.

▶**Marine Turtles**
Endangered marine turtles are highlighted on this WWF site.

▶**Marine Turtles and Ancient Peoples**
Learn more about zooarcheology from this National Zoo site.

Report Links

The Internet sites described below can be accessed at
http://www.myreportlinks.com

▶**Nesting Sea Turtles and Costa Rica's Tropical Rainforest**
View pictures of nesting sea turtles in Tortuguero.

▶**New Marine Conservation Area to Span Four Nations**
Can a protected ocean park help threatened species?

▶**The Ocean Conservancy**
The Ocean Conservancy is committed to protecting the world's oceans and marine life.

▶**Office of Protected Resources: Marine Turtles**
This government site incorporates some of the latest data on sea turtles.

▶**Orientation and Navigation of Sea Turtles**
Information on sea turtle migration is offered.

▶**Pro Peninsula**
This unique conservation organization works to protect the Baja California peninsula.

▶**Sea Turtle Research Program**
Turtle videos and information are available on this NOAA research site.

▶**Sea Turtle Restoration Project**
The goal of this group is to protect endangered sea turtles from extinction.

▶**Seaturtle.org**
This organization helps protect and conserve sea turtles.

▶**Sea Turtles**
Read an online book about sea turtles.

▶**Turtle Excluder Devices (TEDs)**
Read about an inexpensive way to keep sea turtles from being caught in nets.

▶**USFWS Endangered Species Program Kids Corner**
This USFWS Web page offers ways you can help save endangered species.

▶**Watamu Turtle Watch**
This organization protects the sea turtles of Kenya's marine environment.

▶**What Is CITES?**
This international agreement aims to stop the illegal trading of endangered species.

▶**World Turtle Trust**
The World Turtle Trust saves sea turtles one project at a time.

beach replenishment—A process in which offshore sand is pumped onto a beach or trucked in to make the beach larger after storms have washed parts of it away.

biodegradable—Capable of being broken down into harmless chemicals in the environment.

carapace—The top part of a turtle's shell.

clutch—The total group of eggs found in a nest.

combined sewer overflows (CSOs)—Discharges from outdated sewer systems in which the same pipe carries storm water runoff and sewage to a treatment plant. During heavy storms, these systems are designed to overflow, dumping wastewater and other pollutants into bodies of water.

dredging—The deepening of a boating channel.

ecotourism—Vacations that focus on wildlife and the natural places in which animals live, while being careful not to harm the animals or their habitat.

fibropapillomatosis (FP)—An often-fatal disease afflicting sea turtles in which tumors grow on the soft tissue, often covering eyes, mouth, neck, or flippers. It may be caused by ocean pollution.

gill nets or drift nets—Large fishing nets that are set free from boats and then float through the sea to be picked up later.

herbivore—An animal that eats only plants.

keratin—A tough but lightweight substance, like human fingernails, that makes up a turtle's shell.

longlines—Heavy baited fishing lines with thousands of hooks that stretch for miles under the sea.

natal beach—The beach where a sea turtle is born and returns to nest.

poaching—The illegal hunting or taking of an animal or plant.

omnivore—An animal that eats plants and animals.

plastron—The belly or bottom part of a turtle's shell.

reptile—A cold-blooded, egg-laying, air-breathing animal with a backbone.

rookery—A place where an animal species, including birds, some mammals, and sea turtles, nests.

satellite telemetry—The automatic measurement and transmission of radio data from remote sources, such as space satellites, to receiving stations for reading and analysis.

scutes—The plates or scales that combine to form the carapace and plastron of a turtle.

sexual maturity—The age at which an animal can first mate.

symbiosis—A relationship between two species that benefits them both over time.

trawler nets—Large nets dragged behind fishing boats.

turtle excluder devices (TEDs)—Mechanisms put on fishing nets that allow fish to be caught while allowing sea turtles to escape.

Chapter 1. The Ocean World of the Green Sea Turtle

1. Osha Gray Davidson, *Fire in the Turtle House: The Green Sea Turtle and the Fate of the Ocean* (New York: Public Affairs, 2001), p. 2.

2. Ibid., p. 64.

3. Ibid., p. 65.

4. Ibid., p. 73.

5. James R. Spotila, *Sea Turtles: A Complete Guide to Their Biology, Behavior, and Conservation* (Baltimore: Johns Hopkins University Press, 2004), p. 218.

Chapter 2. All About Sea Turtles

1. Peter Matthiessen, *Wildlife in America* (New York: The Penguin Group, 1959), p. 273.

2. James R. Spotila, *Sea Turtles: A Complete Guide to Their Biology, Behavior, and Conservation* (Baltimore: Johns Hopkins University Press, 2004), p. 163.

3. Mathiessen, pp. 273–274.

4. Spotila, p. 97.

5. Caribbean Conservation Corporation and Sea Turtle Survival League, "Species Fact Sheet," n.d., <http://www.cccturtle.org/green.htm> (July 7, 2005).

6. Florida Fish and Wildlife Conservation Commission, Fish and Wildlife Research Institute, "Green Sea Turtle 2004 Statewide Nesting Totals," n.d., <http://research.myfwc.com/features/view_article.asp?id=11812> (August 8, 2005).

7. Spotila, p. 43.

8. John A. Murray, *The Islands and the Sea: Five Centuries of Nature Writing from the Caribbean* (New York: Oxford University Press, 1991), p. 250.

9. Ibid., p. 251.

10. Ibid., p. 55.

11. F. Papi et al., "Open-Sea Migration of Magnetically Disturbed Sea Turtles," *Journal of Experimental Biology,* November 15, 2000, vol. 203, issue 22 (London, England: Portland Press Ltd.), p. 3435.

12. M. Timothy O'Keefe, *Sea Turtles: The Watchers' Guide* (Lakeland, Fla.: Larsen's Outdoor Publishing, 1995), p. 28.

Chapter 3. Threats to Green Sea Turtles

1. Hillary Mayell, *National Geographic* News, "Overfishing Long Ago Tied to Modern Ecosystem Collapse," August 7, 2001, <http://news.nationalgeographic.com/news/2001/08/0807_ecollapse.html> (July 7, 2005).

2. Charles Barrett, *National Geographic* magazine, "The Great Barrier Reef and Its Isles," September 1930.

3. Ibid.

4. James R. Spotila, *Sea Turtles: A Complete Guide to Their Biology, Behavior, and Conservation* (Baltimore: Johns Hopkins University Press, 2004), p. 104.

5. "Sea Turtles Killed in Turkey," *Geographical,* November 2001, vol. 73, issue 11, p. 12.

6. Osha Gray Davidson, *Fire in the Turtle House: The Green Sea Turtle and the Fate of the Ocean* (New York: Public Affairs, 2001), p. 159.

Chapter 4. Protecting Green Sea Turtles

1. Osha Gray Davidson, *Fire in the Turtle House: The Green Sea Turtle and the Fate of the Ocean* (New York: Public Affairs, 2001), pp. 65–66.

2. Sea Turtle Restoration Project, "Groups Sue Fisheries Service Again to Protect Endangered Turtles from Longline Hooks," n.d., <http://www.seaturtles.org/press_release2.cfm?pressID=105> (July 7, 2005).

3. United Nations Inter-American Convention for the Protection and Conservation of Sea Turtles, August 27, 1998, <http://www.seaturtle .org/iac/intro.shtml> (July 7, 2005).

4. Watamu Turtle Watch, "Adopt a Sea Turtle," n.d., <http:// www.adoptaseaturtle.com/> (July 7, 2005).

5. Turtle Trax, "A Page Devoted to Marine Turtles," n.d., <http:// www.turtles.org/> (July 7, 2005).

6. U.S. National Marine Fisheries Service, Hawaii Preparatory Academy, and SeeMore Wildlife Systems, "The Amazing Hawaiian SeaTurtleCam," n.d., <http://www.turtles.org/honucam/honucam .htm> (July 7, 2005).

7. Seaturtle.org, "Image Library," n.d., <http://www.seaturtle.org/ imagelib/> (July 7, 2005).

8. Congress.org, "Home Page," n.d., <http://www.congress.org/ congressorg/home/> (July 7, 2005).

9. Earthwatch Institute, "Home Page," n.d., <www.earthwatch .org/> (July 7, 2005).

Chapter 5. The Current Status of Green Sea Turtles

1. World Conservation Union, "Red List," n.d., <http://www .redlist.org/search/details.php?species=4615> (July 7, 2005).

2. James R. Spotila, *Sea Turtles: A Complete Guide to Their Biology, Behavior, and Conservation* (Baltimore: Johns Hopkins University Press, 2004), p. 105.

3. The Sea Turtle Restoration Project, "The Sea Turtles of Central America," <http://www.seaturtles.org/progBackground.cfm ?campaignBackgroundID=27> (July 7, 2005).

4. Tim Padgett, *Time* Magazine Online, "Heroes for the Planet— Peter Pritchard, Tickled About Turtles," March 13, 2000, <http:// www.time.com/time/reports/environment/heroes/heroesgallery/0,296 7,pritchard,00.html>

5. Projeto (Project) Tamar, n.d., <http://www.tamar.org.br/ ingles/default.htm> (July 7, 2005).

6. Caribbean Conservation Corporation and Sea Turtle Survival League, "Tortuguero National Park, Costa Rica, Region of the Turtles," n.d., <www.cccturtle.org/tortnp.htm> (July 7, 2005).

7. Amelia Island Sea Turtle Watch, n.d., <http://www. kayakamelia.com/turtles.html> (July 7, 2005).

8. World Turtle Trust, "Honu Project," n.d., <http:// world-turtle-trust.org/about.html> (July 7, 2005).

9. Sea Turtle Restoration Project, "Sea Turtle Crisis Addressed at UN," March 18, 2005, <http://www.seaturtles.org/press_release2 .cfm?pressID=251> (July 7, 2005).

10. Sea Turtle Restoration Project, "New Report: Saving Sea Turtles Is Good for the Economy," March 9, 2005, <http://www.seaturtles .org/press_release2.cfm?pressID=249> (July 7, 2005).

Chapter 6. Can We Save Green Sea Turtles and the Seas?

1. Osha Gray Davidson, *Fire in the Turtle House: The Green Sea Turtle and the Fate of the Ocean* (New York: Public Affairs, 2001), p. 163.

2. Ibid., p. 48.

3. James R. Spotila, *Sea Turtles: A Complete Guide to Their Biology, Behavior, and Conservation* (Baltimore: John Hopkins University Press, 2004), p. 108.

Further Reading

Bair, Diane, and Pamela Wright. *Sea Turtle Watching.* Mankato, Minn.: Capstone Books, 2000.

Becker, John E. *Green Sea Turtles.* San Diego: Kidhaven Press, 2004.

Carr, Archie Fairly. *So Excellent a Fishe: A Natural History of Sea Turtles.* New York: The Natural History Press, 1967.

Cerullo, Mary M. *Sea Turtles: Ocean Nomads.* New York: Dutton's Children's Books, 2003.

Davidson, Osha Gray. *Fire in the Turtle House: The Green Sea Turtle and the Fate of the Ocean.* New York: Public Affairs, 2001.

Day, Trevor. *Exploring the Oceans.* New York: Oxford University Press, 2003.

Encyclopedia of the Aquatic World. New York: Marshall Cavendish, 2004.

Lasky, Kathryn. *Interrupted Journey: Saving Endangered Sea Turtles.* Cambridge, Mass.: Candlewick Press, 2001.

Orenstein, Ronald. *Turtles, Tortoises, and Terrapins: Survivors in Armor.* Buffalo: Firefly Books, 2001.

Simon, Seymour. *They Swim the Seas: The Mystery of Animal Migration.* San Diego: Harcourt Brace, 1998.

Thomas, Peggy. *Reptile Rescue.* Brookfield, Conn.: Twenty-First Century Books, 2000.